# Everyday Pasta

# Everyday Pasta

Favorite Pasta Recipes for Every Occasion

## giada de laurentiis

Photographs by Victoria Pearson

Clarkson Potter/Publishers
New York

Copyright © 2007 by Giada De Laurentiis
Photographs © 2007 by Victoria Pearson

Published in the United States by Clarkson Potter/Publishers, an imprint
of the Crown Publishing Group, a division of Random House, Inc., New York.
www.crownpublishing.com
www.clarksonpotter.com

Clarkson N. Potter is a trademark and Potter and colophon are registered
trademarks of Random House, Inc.

Library of Congress Cataloging-in-Publication Data
is available upon request.

ISBN 978-0-307-34658-2

Printed in the United States of America

Design by Wayne Wolf/Blue Cup Design

10  9  8  7  6  5  4  3  2  1

First Edition

To my grandfather Dino De Laurentiis, for preserving our heritage and passing down his passion for great food and, more importantly, the love of pasta!

Also by **GIADA DE LAURENTIIS**
Everyday Italian, Giada's Italian Dinners

# Acknowledgments

It takes lots of collaboration to put a cookbook together, so I want to take this opportunity to thank all the people who contributed to *Everyday Pasta*:

**Pam Krauss**, for helping me put my thoughts on paper—and for making the process fun. **Marysarah Quinn**, for all her patience and good design sense. **Jon Rosen**, for helping me make my dreams a reality. **Eric Greenspan**—so much more than my lawyer; I couldn't have a better person looking out for me. **Suzanne Gluck**, the best literary agent around. **Vicki Pearson**, for bringing my food to life. **Rori Trovato**, for all of her patience and creativity. **Kate Martindale**, for giving my food a beautiful backdrop. **Katrina Norwood**, without whom I couldn't get the recipes just right. **Sandra Tripicchio Corcoran**, for ALL her hard work; I'm not sure I could do all I do without her! **Karen Panoch**, for making me glow. **Christian Navarro**, for teaching all of us about wine. **My family**, for keeping me honest. My husband, **Todd**, without whom none of this would matter. **Food Network**, for all their support. And **Jenny Frost, Lauren Shakely, Philip Patrick, Tina Constable, Kate Tyler, Sydney Webber, Amy Boorstein, Mark McCauslin, Joan Denman, Kathleen Fleury**, and everyone else at Clarkson Potter for their support and guidance!

—OPEN→
SUGO di POMIDORO · MARINARA
San Marzano®
Sauce
©SILtd
San Marzano®
Sauce
©SILtd
(1 LB 10 OZ) 737g
SUGO di POMIDORO · MARINARA

# Contents

# The origins of pasta

are widely disputed, despite the many attempts by food historians to assign it a definitive birthplace.

We now know that pasta did not arrive in Italy courtesy of Marco Polo, who was said to have first encountered it in China; the ancient Romans prepared a dough of water and flour called *lagane* that later came to be referred to as *lasagna*, and many others have laid claim to the invention of pasta. But I've decided to leave the history to scholars and instead focus on pasta as a staple of Italian culture—and in my kitchen.

Pasta has always played a central role in my family, starting in the late 1800s with my great-grandfather Rosario Pasquale Aurelio De Laurentiis, who was a pasta maker in Naples, Italy.

In the early 1900s he enlisted his children, one of them being my grandfather Dino De Laurentiis, to sell the pasta door-to-door as a means of supporting the family. Dino left home when he was seventeen to make movies, but he continued to express his love of pasta and Italian cuisine when he launched the restaurant/marketplace concept called DDL Foodshow, which opened in both New York City and Beverly Hills in the 1980s. When I wasn't happily feasting on the quick pasta dishes my mother was whipping up, I was hanging out at the restaurant with my grandfather and his amazing Italian chefs, watching closely as they made fresh spaghetti and raviolis. These early experiences in the kitchens of DDL Foodshow and helping my mother prepare our family meals are what encouraged me to pursue a culinary career, and continue the traditions of my grandfather.

I have always considered pasta one of the great pleasures of the table; it's healthy and delicious; it can be light and delicate or incredibly hearty; it's readily available; and it's generally very easy to prepare—everything you want in a meal! So when the low-carb craze hit the American food culture with a vengeance, it was disheartening to see pasta singled out as one of the ultimate dietary evils. The truth is, pasta itself contains virtually no fat, and, eaten in moderation, it is quite low in calories. The real culprit is the supersized portions we've all come to regard as normal. Any food consumed in large quantities is unhealthy, regardless of its carbohydrate content. A slice of bread with butter won't make you fat; half a loaf will.

Luckily, America has recognized that a carb-free diet is unrealistic in so many ways and that a healthy portion of pasta—about two to four ounces—can be tasty *and* filling. Since most of our schedules give us little free time to do much of *anything,* much less cook, pasta offers an easy solution when we need a quick meal that is also good for us and, most importantly, tastes amazing.

Pasta (which means "paste" in Italian) is simply semolina (durum wheat flour) combined with water or milk to create a dough that can be transformed into literally hundreds of sizes, shapes, colors, and flavors. I grew up eating penne, spaghetti, rigatoni, pastina, and orecchiette, and over the years I have expanded the list of favorites to include fettuccine, fusilli, farfalle, orzo, and wheat pasta, among others.

In fresh pasta, the liquid is replaced by eggs for a richer, more delicate flavor that is a real treat, especially with cream-based sauces like a béchamel. I have provided a very easy recipe on page 222 for those who would like to try their hands at making fresh pasta, something I urge you to do if you have some time (and a pasta rolling machine!). However, even if you don't make your own, it is now easy to find fresh pasta at gourmet specialty stores and even the supermarket, so do add it to your repertoire.

With so many varieties of pasta cuts and flavors available, it isn't difficult to be creative when deciding upon a dish. Pasta provides a perfect neutral canvas on which to combine flavors and ingredients. It can be warming and comforting when the days are cool, and light and fresh tasting when the temperatures rise. It's a perfect showcase for fresh seasonal vegetables, and an inexpensive way to stretch a little bit of a costly ingredient like seafood or exotic mushrooms to feed a group. Many pasta dishes are all-in-one meal that, at most, need a quick, easy vegetable side dish or perhaps a simple appetizer to round them out (see pages 21–59 for some of my favorite sides, salads, and bread accompaniments for pasta meals). Best of all, nearly all the recipes in this book can be assembled in the time it takes to bring water to a boil and cook the pasta, and many of those that are a bit more involved can be made ahead and reheated or served at room temperature. When you have a well-stocked pantry of ingredients such as olive oil, tomato paste, whole canned tomatoes, anchovies, parsley, basil, garlic, lemons, and olives, you're already halfway to a great pasta meal.

The other half has to do with preparing your pasta properly and maximizing its full texture and flavor. I always tell people that there's nothing to be afraid of when cooking pasta. It's practically failsafe if you follow a few simple rules. First and foremost, pasta should always be cooked in a large pot with plenty of generously salted, boiling water to allow the noodles to swim freely, releasing their starches and cooking evenly. Your pasta should be al dente or "to the tooth," which means that when you take a bite of your cooked pasta, it should still offer slight resistance. Remember: residual heat will continue to cook the pasta even after it's drained, whether it is transferred into a hot sauce or left to cool at room temperature. Don't ever rinse your pasta unless you're making a pasta salad; the starches add flavor and help the sauce adhere to the noodles. And finally, always reserve a half cup or so of the cooking water before you drain the pasta to add to the sauce. The starch in the water will add flavor and help the sauce stick to the noodles. It's my secret to any good pasta sauce.

I wanted to write this book as a way of sharing with you the central role pasta has played in my family—as it has in the lives of most Italian families. When we gather around the table, there is always a pasta dish in the center.

When I open my pantry, there's always pasta, and when I think about Italian food, I see pasta. If you already love pasta, I hope these recipes will make you love it more; and if you're just embarking on the pasta journey, I think you'll quickly see what all the fuss is about.

# Giada's top 10
# Pasta-Cooking Tips

**1.** Always cook pasta in a big-enough pot; one that is tall and deep rather than wide and shallow is best for long strands.

**2.** Use a generous amount of water; the pasta should be able to swim freely in the pot.

**3.** Salt the water with a good handful of kosher or sea salt; this is really your only chance to season the pasta itself (and not just the sauce), and salt brings out the flavor of any pasta.

**4.** Never rinse cooked pasta; the starch on the surface contributes flavor and helps the sauce adhere. The only exception to this rule is pasta for cold salads, which will be too sticky and gummy when the noodles cool unless some of the surface starch is rinsed off.

**5.** Always reserve a quarter cup or so of the pasta cooking water to add to the sauce. This both loosens the sauce so it can coat the pasta and contributes starch that helps it cling better.

**6.** Don't add olive oil to the pasta cooking water. It is an old wives' tale that this will keep it from sticking as it cooks; pasta clumps together when it is not cooked in sufficient water. Save your olive oil for salad dressing.

**7.** Don't coat drained pasta with olive oil to keep it from sticking; this will prevent the sauce from clinging to the pasta, causing it to end up in a pool at the bottom of your serving dish.

**8.** Cook the pasta just to al dente and no longer; start testing it a minute or two before the time indicated on the package to make sure it doesn't overcook. The pasta should still offer definite resistance when you bite it but not be pasty white or hard inside.

**9.** Remember that your pasta will continue to cook when you add it to the hot sauce and toss them together, so don't leave it in the pan any longer than necessary to marry the sauce and pasta together and warm them both through.

**10.** Lastly, keep portion sizes reasonable! A cup of cooked pasta is plenty for a first course or appetizer serving.

# Matching Pasta Shapes to Sauce:
# A Basic Primer

Although the flavor of pasta doesn't vary much, whether it's a short cut like farfalle or a long strand like linguine, the way these shapes interact with sauce makes a big difference in the finished dish. Here's an overview of several popular shapes and which sauces they are best suited to.

**Capellini and angel-hair pasta:** Because the noodles are long and thin, these pastas go best with a light sauce that won't weigh down the pasta. Try it with olive oil, garlic, and lemon, or a simple tomato-basil sauce.

**Spaghetti:** The most famous cut of pasta, it pairs nicely with simple sauces like tomato, arrabbiata, or puttanesca or with seafood and herbs.

**Linguine:** These long, flat pasta strands stand up to sturdier sauces. Typical matches would be a pesto, tomato, or mushroom sauce, or one with flavorful ingredients like shellfish.

**Fettuccine:** Literally these are "little ribbons," similar to linguine but thicker and wider. It is a suitable match for many sauces, including those that are cream-based or made with meat.

**Farfalle:** These pretty butterfly shapes taste best with simple olive oil- or tomato-based sauces that may incorporate ingredients such as peppers, chicken, or arugula. They are also great for a pasta salad because the shape is fun and bite-sized.

**Rotelle:** Shaped like wagon wheels, rotelle are popular with kids. I serve them with an artichoke pesto, but they can also be dressed with bolognese or a hearty tomato sauce with sun-dried tomatoes, olives, and capers.

**Fusilli bucati:** Similar to fusilli, which look like corkscrews, these noodles look more like bedsprings. They are a good choice for thick and hearty sauces because all the "goodness" gets trapped inside the spiral rather than just coating the exterior.

**Elbows:** A classic for mac and cheese, this basic shape is also perfect with sour cream– or mayonnaise-based sauces for pasta salads.

**Conchiglie (shells):** These come in various sizes, from very large ones meant for stuffing, to very small ones, which are called conchigliette. Shells are good with meat sauces, and the small ones work in any dish where you'd use elbow macaroni.

**Rigatoni:** This wide, ridged, tube-shaped pasta has holes on either end that are large enough to capture pieces of meat or vegetables in a sauce. In addition, this kind of pasta is perfect for baked dishes made with sauce and cheese.

**Penne:** These small tubes may be smooth or ridged (rigate). Penne is best used in soups, pasta salads, and with thicker sauces and casseroles, as the ingredients and sauces can penetrate the inside of the pasta. Penne rigate is ideal for meat, vegetable, or butter-and-oil-based sauces because the ridges hold the sauce.

pasta

# go-withs

# 1

# antipasti and appetizers

Most pasta meals, because they are generally relaxed even last-minute affairs, don't seem to need a formal, plated first course. When I serve pasta to a group, or even just my family, I am much more likely to set out a few antipasti for people to nibble on than to prepare a separate appetizer course to serve at the table. Generally I make just one or two items, like a bruschetta or crostini, or perhaps some pickled vegetables, and arrange them on a board with sliced meats and cheese from the deli and pantry items like olives, marinated artichokes, pepperoncini, and roasted peppers. That way people can stave off hunger pangs and keep me company while I work in the kitchen, but no one gets too full and I don't have to clear the table for the main event. Any of the recipes in this chapter would be welcome additions to an antipasto platter and equally nice to serve with a bowl of soup to make it a bit more of a meal.

# antipasti and appetizers

Baked Caprese Salad

Goat Cheese Toasts

Bruschetta with Frisée, Prosciutto, and Mozzarella

Toasted Ciabatta with Balsamic Syrup

Crostini with Anchovy Butter and Cheese

Parmesan Popovers

Fried Ravioli

Zucchini and Carrot a Scapece

Fried Zucchini

Prosciutto-Wrapped Vegetables with Parmesan

# Baked Caprese Salad

4 to 6 servings

Be careful not to overheat the crostini; the cheese and tomatoes should be just warmed through and softened but not melted or falling apart. It's perfect if you have slightly underripe tomatoes.

| | |
|---|---|
| 1 | baguette, sliced ½ inch thick (30 to 36 slices) |
| ¼ | cup extra-virgin olive oil |
| | Salt |
| 5 | Roma tomatoes, sliced |
| | Freshly ground black pepper |
| 1¼ | pounds fresh mozzarella cheese, sliced |
| | Leaves from 1 bunch of fresh basil |

Preheat the oven to 450°F. Arrange the baguette slices on a baking sheet, brush with some of the olive oil, and sprinkle with salt. Bake until the bread is pale golden and crisp, about 5 minutes. Top each slice of bread with a slice of tomato and sprinkle with salt and pepper. Top with a slice of mozzarella cheese and sprinkle with salt. Return the baking sheet to the oven until the cheese and tomato are just warm, about 5 minutes.

Arrange the toasts on a serving platter. Top each toast with a basil leaf. Using the brush, drizzle the remaining olive oil over the basil. Sprinkle with salt and pepper, and serve.

# Goat Cheese Toasts

6 servings

Goat cheese is something I like to use in many different ways, and this herb-y mixture is especially versatile. You can toss it with hot pasta for a quick, creamy sauce, or roll it into balls to top a salad, but I probably like these little toasts best of all. They're so easy to make and they fly off the platter every time I serve them. The recipe can easily be doubled for a party. (See photograph, page 24.)

| | |
|---|---|
| 1 | baguette, cut on the diagonal in 18 half-inch slices |
| 3 | tablespoons olive oil |
| 4 | ounces soft fresh goat cheese |
| 2 | ounces cream cheese |
| 1 | teaspoon finely chopped fresh flat-leaf parsley |
| 1 | teaspoon finely chopped fresh thyme |
| 1 | teaspoon finely grated lemon zest |
| | Salt and coarsely ground multicolored or black peppercorns |
| ¼ | cup pitted Sicilian green olives or kalamata olives, finely chopped |
| 1 | tablespoon finely chopped chives |

Preheat the oven to 375°F. Arrange the bread slices on one or two large, heavy baking sheets. Brush the olive oil over the bread slices. Bake until the crostini are pale golden and crisp, about 10 to 15 minutes.

Blend the goat cheese and cream cheese in a food processor until smooth and creamy. Add the parsley, thyme, and lemon zest. Pulse just to blend. Season to taste with salt and pepper. Spread the cheese mixture over the crostini. Sprinkle with the olives, chives, and more pepper. Arrange the toasts on a platter and serve.

**Do-Ahead Tip**
The crostini and cheese mixture can be prepared 2 days ahead. Store the crostini in an airtight container at room temperature. Cover and refrigerate the cheese mixture. Let the cheese mixture stand at room temperature for 1 hour to soften slightly before spreading.

# Bruschetta with Frisée, Prosciutto, and Mozzarella

6 servings

Think of this bruschetta as a portable salad that doesn't require utensils or a plate—perfect for entertaining! (See photograph, page 24.)

| | |
|---|---|
| 1 | baguette, cut on the diagonal in 18 half-inch slices |
| 3 | tablespoons olive oil |
| 18 | paper-thin slices prosciutto |
| 1 | (8-ounce) ball of fresh mozzarella, cut into 18 thin slices |
| 1 | head of frisée, leaves separated |
| 2 | tablespoons Red Wine Vinaigrette (page 229) |

Preheat the oven to 375°F. Arrange the bread slices on one or two large, heavy baking sheets and brush with the olive oil. Bake until the crostini are pale golden and crisp, about 10 to 15 minutes.

Place one slice of prosciutto on a work surface. Place a slice of cheese and 2 or 3 frisée leaves on top, allowing the tops to protrude from one end. Roll the prosciutto around the cheese and frisée and place on a toasted bread slice. Repeat with the remaining ingredients.

Arrange the crostini on a platter. Drizzle with the vinaigrette and serve.

# Toasted Ciabatta with Balsamic Syrup

6 servings

I love this sweet syrup. It's similar to chocolate sauce; in fact, beyond the antipasto platter, you could even use it as a dessert topping, drizzled over ice cream or berries.

| | |
|---|---|
| 1½ | cups balsamic vinegar |
| 4 | tablespoons sugar |
| 12 | ½-inch-thick slices ciabatta bread |
| 2 | tablespoons unsalted butter, softened |

Boil the balsamic vinegar and 3 tablespoons of sugar in a small, heavy saucepan over medium-high heat until reduced to ½ cup, stirring occasionally, about 20 minutes.

Toast the bread slices. Spread the butter over the toasts. Arrange the toasts on a platter. Drizzle the reduced balsamic syrup over the toasts, then sprinkle with the remaining tablespoon of sugar, and serve.

# Crostini with Anchovy Butter and Cheese

Makes 24

Garlic bread done even better: the salty, buttery, garlicky topping makes these toasts absolutely addictive.

| | |
|---|---|
| ¼ | cup (½ stick) unsalted butter |
| 4 | anchovy fillets, drained and chopped |
| 2 | tablespoons chopped fresh flat-leaf parsley |
| 1 | teaspoon chopped fresh thyme |
| 1 | teaspoon minced garlic |
| ½ | teaspoon minced lemon zest |
| ¼ | teaspoon crushed red pepper flakes |
| 12 | ½-inch-thick baguette slices |
| 1 | cup shredded Provolone cheese |

Melt the butter in a small, heavy skillet over medium heat. Add the anchovies and stir until they dissolve, about 3 minutes. Stir in the parsley, thyme, garlic, lemon zest, and crushed red pepper flakes.

Preheat the oven to 425°F. Arrange the bread slices on a large baking sheet. Brush with the anchovy mixture, then sprinkle with the cheese. Bake until the cheese melts and the bread is golden, about 10 minutes.

# Parmesan Popovers

*Irresistible* is the only word for these light and airy popovers. Add them to the bread basket with dinner or lunch and see how quickly they disappear. (See photograph, page 44.)

| | |
|---|---|
| 6 | eggs |
| 1½ | cups all-purpose flour |
| ¼ | teaspoon salt |
| ½ | teaspoon freshly ground black pepper |
| ½ | teaspoon herbes de Provence |
| ¼ | cup chopped fresh flat-leaf parsley |
| 2 | cups whole milk |
| 1¼ | cups grated Parmesan cheese (about 5 ounces) |

Preheat the oven to 400°F.

In a blender, combine the eggs, flour, salt, pepper, herbes de Provence, and parsley. Blend on medium speed. Turn the blender to low and slowly add the milk, then the cheese.

Spray a muffin pan with nonstick cooking spray. Pour the batter into the muffin cups, filling each cup three-quarters full. Bake until puffed and golden brown, 20 to 25 minutes.

Remove the popovers from the muffin pan and serve hot, or cool on a wire rack and serve warm or at room temperature.

# Fried Ravioli

4 to 6 servings

When I visited St. Louis on my first book tour, I sampled these addictive little cocktail nibbles. They are a perfect addition to an antipasto platter or a fun and easy party appetizer; serve them on a big platter with a small bowl of marinara in the center for dipping.

|   | Olive oil, for frying |
|---|---|
| 1 | cup buttermilk |
| 2 | cups Italian-style bread crumbs |
| 1 | box store-bought bite-size cheese ravioli (about 24 ravioli) |
| ¼ | cup freshly grated Parmesan cheese |
| 1 | to 2 cups marinara sauce (store-bought or homemade; see page 224), heated, for dipping |

Heat 2 inches of olive oil in a large frying pan over medium heat until a deep-fry thermometer registers 325°F.

While the oil is heating, put the buttermilk and the bread crumbs in separate shallow bowls. Working in batches, dip the ravioli in the buttermilk to coat completely, allowing the excess buttermilk to drip back into the bowl. Dredge the ravioli in the bread crumbs. Place the ravioli on a baking sheet, while you coat the remaining ravioli.

When the oil is hot, fry the ravioli in batches, turning occasionally, until golden brown, about 3 minutes. Using a slotted spoon, transfer the fried ravioli to paper towels to drain.

Sprinkle the fried ravioli with Parmesan cheese and serve with a bowl of warmed marinara sauce for dipping.

# Zucchini and Carrot a Scapece

6 servings

*A scapece* means pickled, and the longer the vegetables marinate in the red wine vinegar, the better they taste. My family used to make them in the winter when the veggies weren't at their peak. These are super versatile; serve them alongside pasta, bread, fish, or meat or as the center-piece of an antipasto platter.

| | |
|---|---|
| 6 | tablespoons extra-virgin olive oil |
| 5 | large zucchini (about 2 pounds), cut in ¼-inch rounds |
| | Salt and freshly ground black pepper |
| 3 | garlic cloves, thinly sliced |
| ¼ | cup fresh basil leaves, chopped |
| ¼ | cup fresh mint leaves, chopped |
| 10 | medium carrots (about 1 pound), peeled and cut in ¼-inch rounds |
| ¼ | cup red wine vinegar |

Heat 3 tablespoons of the oil in a large, heavy frying pan over medium-high heat. Working in batches, add the zucchini slices and fry until golden, about 2 minutes per side. Use a slotted spoon to transfer the fried zucchini to a baking dish. Sprinkle generously with salt and pepper, then with half of the garlic, basil, and mint.

Add the remaining 3 tablespoons of oil to the frying pan. Add the carrots to the hot oil and sauté until golden, about 5 minutes. Use a slotted spoon to add the fried carrots to the dish with the zucchini. Sprinkle generously with salt and pepper and the remaining garlic, basil, and mint. Drizzle the vinegar over the vegetable mixture and toss gently to coat. Cool to room temperature, then cover and marinate at room temperature for 8 hours, or overnight in the refrigerator. (Allow the vegetables to come to room temperature before serving.) Transfer the scapece to a platter and serve at room temperature.

# Fried Zucchini

4 servings

In Naples, fried zucchini is a street food, and it was always my favorite component of Frito Misto (a dish of mixed fried foods) when I was a child. I've made it lighter by coating it in the Japanese bread crumbs called *panko* instead of regular bread crumbs, a method you could use equally well with sweet potato slices, carrots, broccoli, cauliflower, peppers—really any vegetable you like.

1¾ cups freshly grated Parmesan cheese

1½ cups panko (Japanese bread crumbs)

¾ teaspoon salt

2 large eggs

3 medium zucchini, cut into ½-inch strips

Olive oil, for deep-frying

Stir 1½ cups of the Parmesan cheese, the panko, and salt together in a medium bowl to blend. Whisk the eggs in another medium bowl to break them up. Working in batches, dip the zucchini sticks in the eggs to coat them completely, allowing the excess egg to drip back into the bowl. Coat the zucchini in the panko mixture, patting to adhere and coat completely. Place the coated zucchini strips on a baking sheet.

Heat 2 inches of oil in a large frying pan over medium heat until a deep-fry thermometer registers 350°F. Working in batches, fry the zucchini sticks until they are golden brown, about 3 minutes. Use a slotted spoon to transfer the fried zucchini to paper towels and drain.

Arrange the fried zucchini on a platter. Sprinkle with the remaining ¼ cup of Parmesan cheese and serve.

# Prosciutto-Wrapped Vegetables with Parmesan

4 to 6 servings

It's time to reinvent the crudité platter, and I nominate these attractive little bundles of vegetables; they're great with cocktails for entertaining as an alternative to a boring deli plate, but they are also a nice alternative to a salad with a pasta dinner. My friends request this often.

| | |
|---|---|
| 6 | broccolini stalks |
| 6 | small cauliflower florets with stems |
| 15 | paper-thin slices prosciutto |
| ½ | fennel bulb, trimmed, cored, and thinly sliced lengthwise |
| ½ | orange bell pepper, cored, seeded, and cut lengthwise into thin strips |
| ½ | red bell pepper, cored, seeded, and cut lengthwise into thin strips |
| | 2-ounce piece of Parmesan cheese |
| 2 | tablespoons Meyer lemon olive oil |

Bring a medium pot of salted water to a boil over high heat. Place a large bowl of ice water near the stove. Cook the broccolini in the boiling water for 1 minute, then use a slotted spoon to transfer it to the bowl of ice water. Let cool for 2 minutes, then drain on a towel and reserve. Cook the cauliflower in the boiling water for 3 minutes, then cool in the ice water and drain as for the broccolini.

Working with 1 slice at a time, cut the prosciutto slices in half lengthwise. Make a small bundle of fennel slices and wrap it with prosciutto, allowing the fennel to extend out the ends. Bundle together 2 strips each of orange and red bell peppers and wrap them with prosciutto in the same way. Wrap prosciutto strips around the stalks of broccolini and the stem ends of the cauliflower florets.

Using a vegetable peeler, shave the Parmesan cheese onto a large platter or serving plates; arrange the vegetable bundles over the cheese shavings. Drizzle the oil over the bundles.

# 2

# something on the side

One of the great things about many pasta dishes is that they are an all-in-one meal—starch, vegetables, and maybe some protein conveniently dished up at once. Sometimes, though, it's nice to augment your pasta with a little something more: a salad to start or finish the meal or a quick vegetable side to complement a pasta dish that doesn't feature many vegetables. I believe in *always* serving some kind of green when serving a pasta. It rounds out the meal and cleans the palate. Italians serve salad after the main course, but these can also be served before. These are some of my favorite dishes to serve with pasta and none of them takes more than a few minutes to put together. Most of the recipes in this chapter would work well as a first course for a more formal dinner, too. And when you're serving a baked or cheesy pasta, a side of sautéed spinach or a mixed green salad lightens the meal and ensures everyone gets a serving of veggies.

# something on the side

Cornbread Panzanella

Arugula Salad with Fried Gorgonzola

Spinach Salad with Citrus Vinaigrette

Insalata Mista with Basil Dressing

Hearty Winter Salad with Sherry Vinaigrette

Greens with Gorgonzola Dressing

Asparagus with Vin Santo Vinaigrette

Anytime Vegetable Salad

Sautéed Spinach with Red Onion

# Cornbread Panzanella

Panzanella is a staple of Tuscan cooking that is traditionally made with leftover stale bread; the dressing moistens the bread, which soaks in all the flavors and juices from the vegetables. I like panzanella but I *love* cornbread. When I found myself with lots of leftover cornbread one Thanksgiving, I was inspired to give it an Italian spin, and this salad was born.

It's best to use stale cornbread, but if you have only fresh cornbread, toast the cubes in the oven at 300°F for 8 to 10 minutes to dry them out; that way they won't fall apart in the salad and become mushy.

| | |
|---|---|
| 1 | pound cornbread, cut into 2¾-inch cubes (about 4 cups) |
| 1 | cup halved cherry tomatoes |
| 1 | cup cubed fontina cheese (about ½-inch cubes) |
| ½ | hothouse cucumber, quartered and sliced |
| ½ | cup chopped fresh basil |

**Dressing**

| | |
|---|---|
| ⅔ | cup extra-virgin olive oil |
| | Zest of 1 lemon |
| | Juice of 2 lemons |
| 1 | teaspoon kosher salt |
| 1 | teaspoon freshly ground black pepper |

Combine the cornbread, tomatoes, cheese, cucumber, and basil in a large bowl.

In a small bowl, combine the olive oil, lemon zest and juice, salt, and pepper. Stir together and pour over the salad. Toss very gently to combine. Serve immediately.

# Arugula Salad with Fried Gorgonzola

6 servings

Little fried balls of Gorgonzola turn a boring green salad into a mouthful of joy. For convenience, you can prepare and chill the cheese balls overnight so they are very firm before you fry them. To test the temperature of your oil, drop a small piece of bread into the pot. If it sinks to the bottom, the oil is not hot enough; if it rises slowly to the top and turns golden brown, it's just right for frying.

| | |
|---|---|
| 7 | ounces Gorgonzola cheese |
| 1 | large egg |
| ¾ | cup dried bread crumbs |
| ½ | teaspoon grated lemon zest |
| 3 | tablespoons freshly squeezed lemon juice |
| 1 | garlic clove, minced |
| ⅓ | cup olive oil, plus more for deep-frying |
| | Salt and freshly ground black pepper |
| 2 | (10-ounce) bags of arugula, coarsely torn (about 12 cups) |

Blend the Gorgonzola cheese in a food processor until smooth and creamy, scraping down the sides of the work bowl occasionally. Break the egg into a shallow dish and beat lightly to blend; put the bread crumbs in a second shallow dish. Using 1 rounded teaspoon of cheese for each, form the cheese into eighteen 1-inch balls. Working in batches, coat the balls with the beaten egg then with the bread crumbs. Arrange the balls on a small baking sheet. Cover and refrigerate until cold, at least 1 hour or overnight.

Whisk the lemon zest, lemon juice, and garlic in a medium bowl to blend. Gradually whisk in the ⅓ cup of oil. Season the dressing to taste with salt and pepper.

Heat 2 inches of oil in a small, heavy saucepan over medium heat. Working in batches, add the balls to the hot oil and fry just until golden brown, about 20 seconds. Using a slotted spoon, transfer the fried balls to paper towels to drain.

Toss the arugula in a large bowl with enough dressing to coat the leaves. Season the salad to taste with salt and pepper. Mound the salad on plates and top each serving with a few of the hot fried Gorgonzola balls. Serve immediately.

# Spinach Salad with Citrus Vinaigrette

4 to 6 servings

When I make a salad I like to bring in lots of different textures and flavors. This one has citrus for zing, herbs for freshness, and nuts for crunch. The citrus vinaigrette cuts through the raw spinach flavor.

**Citrus Vinaigrette**

| | |
|---|---|
| 1/2 | cup extra-virgin olive oil |
| 1 | teaspoon grated lemon zest |
| 1 | teaspoon grated orange zest |
| 2 | tablespoons freshly squeezed lemon juice |
| 1 | tablespoon freshly squeezed orange juice |
| 1 | teaspoon fresh thyme leaves, chopped |
| 1 | teaspoon honey |
| 1/2 | teaspoon salt |
| 1/4 | teaspoon freshly ground black pepper |

**Spinach Salad**

| | |
|---|---|
| 1 | (10-ounce) bag of spinach (about 6 cups) |
| 2 | oranges, cut into segments (see Note) |
| 1/2 | cup sliced almonds, toasted (see page 168) |
| 1/2 | red onion, thinly sliced |
| | Salt and freshly ground black pepper |
| | Parmesan Frico (page 229) |

Combine all the ingredients for the Citrus Vinaigrette in a jar or a tight-sealing plastic container. Shake to blend.

Combine the spinach, orange segments, almonds, red onion, salt, and pepper in a large bowl. Toss with the Citrus Vinaigrette. Serve on individual plates, topped with 1 or 2 Parmesan Frico.

Note: To cut orange segments, first use a small sharp knife to cut off the top and bottom of the orange. Stand the orange on one of the cut ends and make long, straight cuts to slice away all of the peel and white pith. Hold the peeled orange in your palm and cut on each side of the membranes to free the segments.

# Insalata Mista with Basil Dressing

6 to 8 servings

The dressing is what makes this salad: it's sooo delicious I use it to marinate chicken and fish, drizzle it on pasta salads, or even toss some with boiled new potatoes to make an Italian potato salad. When you make it, double or triple the quantity so you'll always have it on hand to toss with your favorite foods.

| | |
|---|---|
| $1/3$ | cup lightly packed fresh basil leaves |
| $1/3$ | cup white wine vinegar or freshly squeezed lemon juice |
| 1 | teaspoon salt, plus more for seasoning |
| $1/2$ | teaspoon freshly ground black pepper, plus more for seasoning |
| $1/2$ | cup extra-virgin olive oil |
| 8 | cups arugula, torn into small pieces if large |
| 4 | cups bite-size pieces of radicchio (from one 10-ounce head) |
| 1 | carrot, peeled |
| 1 | hothouse (European) cucumber, peeled |

Blend the basil, vinegar, 1 teaspoon of salt, and $1/2$ teaspoon of pepper in a blender. With the machine running, gradually blend in the oil.

Place the arugula and radicchio in a wide, shallow bowl. Using a vegetable peeler, shave the carrot over the salad. Shave the cucumber into a medium bowl and pat the shavings with paper towels to absorb the excess moisture. Add the cucumbers to the salad.

Toss the salad with enough basil dressing to coat. Season to taste with salt and pepper, and serve.

**Do-Ahead Tip**
The vinaigrette and salad can be prepared one day ahead. Cover separately and refrigerate. Whisk or shake the dressing to blend before using.

# Hearty Winter Salad with Sherry Vinaigrette

4 to 6 servings

I make this salad most often in the winter and early spring months, when there aren't a lot of vegetables in the market. The olives and cheese make it a bit more substantial than most green salads.

Sherry vinegar is the special ingredient in the versatile dressing. It's Spain's version of balsamic vinegar and it's less acidic than other vinegars with a mellow, sweet-and-sour taste that is just perfect with more delicate greens.

Dressing

| | |
|---|---|
| 3 | tablespoons sherry vinegar |
| 1 | large garlic clove |
| 1 | teaspoon dried oregano |
| ½ | teaspoon salt |
| ½ | teaspoon freshly ground black pepper |
| ¼ | cup extra-virgin olive oil |

| | |
|---|---|
| 1 | (10-ounce) bag of mixed baby greens, rinsed and spun dry (about 6 cups) |
| 1 | red bell pepper, cored, seeded, and diced |
| ½ | cup pitted kalamata olives, halved |
| 2 | ounces feta cheese, coarsely crumbled |

Blend the vinegar, garlic, oregano, salt, and pepper in a blender until the garlic is finely chopped. With the motor running, slowly blend in the oil.

Toss the baby greens, bell pepper, olives, and cheese in a salad bowl. Drizzle with the dressing and toss to coat.

# Greens with Gorgonzola Dressing

4 to 6 servings

This is the Italian version of blue cheese dressing, and it's just as rich and decadent as its American counterpart.

| | |
|---|---|
| ¼ | cup creamy Gorgonzola cheese (about 2 ounces) |
| ¼ | cup milk |
| 2 | tablespoons sour cream |
| ½ | garlic clove, minced |
| ¼ | teaspoon salt |
| ¼ | teaspoon freshly ground black pepper |
| 10 | ounces bibb, iceberg, or Romaine lettuce in bite-size pieces (about 6 cups) |

Combine all the ingredients except the greens in a blender or a food processor. Pulse a few times to combine, then blend until smooth.

Place the greens in a salad bowl and pour the dressing over the greens. Toss to coat and serve immediately.

# Asparagus with Vin Santo Vinaigrette

4 to 6 servings

Vin Santo is known as the Wine of Saints, and some of the very best is produced in northern Italy. It's drunk mostly as a dessert wine (it's perfect for dipping biscotti), but I also like to use it in vinaigrettes because of its smooth, sweet flavor. It brightens up the asparagus and makes this simple salad more luxurious.

| | |
|---|---|
| 1½ | cups Vin Santo (about 375 milliliters) |
| ⅓ | cup extra-virgin olive oil |
| 1 | tablespoon freshly squeezed lemon juice |
| 1 | tablespoon Dijon mustard |
| ¼ | teaspoon salt |
| ¼ | teaspoon freshly ground black pepper |
| 1 | bunch of asparagus, trimmed |
| 6 | Bibb lettuce leaves |
| 1 | hard-cooked egg, peeled and chopped |
| ¼ | cup chopped toasted almonds (see page 168) |

In a small saucepan, reduce the Vin Santo to ⅓ cup over medium heat, about 10 minutes. In a small jar or plastic container with a tight-fitting lid, combine the reduced Vin Santo, olive oil, lemon juice, mustard, salt, and pepper. Shake to combine, making sure the mustard is fully incorporated.

Bring a large pot of salted water to a boil over high heat. Add the asparagus and cook until just tender, about 3 minutes. Transfer the asparagus to a bowl filled with ice water and let it cool, about 3 minutes. Drain the asparagus and pat dry with paper towels.

Place the lettuce leaves in a serving bowl and arrange the asparagus on top. Top with the hard-cooked egg and chopped almonds. Drizzle the entire salad with the vinaigrette. Serve immediately.

# Anytime Vegetable Salad
4 to 6 servings

The perfect light, clean side salad to serve alongside a hearty pasta, this is my version of succotash. The different shades of yellow and green beans make it really pretty, too.

| | |
|---|---|
| 2 | cups frozen edamame (soy beans), shelled |
| 8 | ounces thin green beans, trimmed |
| 8 | ounces yellow wax beans, trimmed |
| 1/3 | cup red wine vinegar |
| 1 | teaspoon salt, plus more to taste |
| 3/4 | teaspoon freshly ground black pepper, plus more to taste |
| 3 | tablespoons extra-virgin olive oil |
| 1 1/2 | cups halved cherry tomatoes |
| 2 | teaspoons chopped fresh basil or tarragon |
| 2 | teaspoons chopped fresh thyme leaves |

Cook the edamame in a large pot of boiling water until crisp-tender, about 3 minutes. Drain. Rinse under cold water, then drain well and pat dry. Repeat with the green beans and yellow beans. Leave the green and yellow beans whole or cut them crosswise into 1- to 1 1/2-inch pieces.

Whisk the vinegar, salt, and pepper together in a large bowl. Gradually whisk in the oil. Add the beans, tomatoes, basil, and thyme, and toss to coat. Season the salad to taste with more salt and pepper, and serve.

# Sautéed Spinach with Red Onion

4 to 6 servings

I make this as a side dish at least three times a week—that's how much I love spinach, and how much I love it served this way. It's easy, delicious, and great for you. The secret is the soy sauce; although it's not Italian, it gives the spinach a fabulous salty kick.

| | |
|---|---|
| 3 | tablespoons extra-virgin olive oil |
| 1 | large red onion, sliced |
| 2 | garlic cloves, minced |
| ¼ | cup reduced-sodium chicken broth |
| 1 | tablespoon soy sauce |
| ¼ | teaspoon crushed red pepper flakes |
| ¼ | teaspoon salt |
| ½ | teaspoon freshly ground black pepper |
| 2 | (10-ounce) bags of prewashed spinach (about 10 cups) |
| | Zest of 1 lemon |

Heat the oil in a very large pot over medium heat. Add the onion and garlic and cook until tender, about 8 minutes. Add the broth, soy sauce, red pepper flakes, salt, and pepper. Add one third of the spinach and cook until it begins to wilt, about 2 minutes. Continue adding the spinach one large handful at a time, sautéing just until it begins to wilt before adding more. Transfer the mixture to a bowl, sprinkle with lemon zest, and serve.

pasta for

all seasons

# 3

# soups and
# pasta salads

This chapter may be the best illustration of just how versatile pasta can be. A little bit of pasta—whether fun small shapes like ditalini or little stars or just broken bits of long-strand pasta like spaghetti or fettuccine—can turn a light vegetable soup into something more substantial and sustaining, making it a meal. Stuffed pastas like tortellini, which can feel a bit heavy when covered in a rich sauce, are magically transformed into a light, elegant starter when served in a flavorful broth. While the classic *tortellini en brodo* is a holiday tradition in many Italian families, mine included, don't let that limit you. Any kind of stuffed pasta in the broth of your choice, may be supplemented with some fresh herbs or bits of vegetable and a grating of cheese, makes a super-quick and easy meal any time of the year.

When temperatures soar, few things are more welcome than a cooling pasta salad. So much more satisfying than a mixed green salad, pasta salads are also a good way to stretch more pricy ingredients like seafood to serve a crowd. Because most are served at room temperature or chilled, pasta salads are a great addition to an entertaining menu; just make them in advance and put them out with the main course. And because sturdy pasta shapes like penne, farfalle, or rotelli can stand up to robust flavors and ingredients better than delicate greens will, these salads are really rib-sticking; you may find that all you need to make these salads a meal is dessert!

# soups and pasta salads

Italian White Bean, Pancetta, and Tortellini Soup

Pasta e Ceci

Italian Vegetable Soup

Tuscan White Bean and Garlic Soup

Ribollita

Tuna, Green Bean, and Orzo Salad

Fusilli Salad with Seared Shrimp and Parsley Sauce

Neapolitan Calamari and Shrimp Salad

Mediterranean Salad

Antipasto Salad

Italian Chicken Salad in Lettuce Cups

# Italian White Bean, Pancetta, and Tortellini Soup

Use either fresh or frozen tortellini for this soup, a twist on the traditional *tortellini en brodo* that is a traditional Christmas dish all over northern Italy. White beans and the pancetta make this one very hearty and even more flavorful.

| | |
|---|---|
| 3 | tablespoons olive oil |
| 4 | ounces pancetta, chopped |
| 3 | large shallots, chopped |
| 1 | carrot, peeled and chopped |
| 2 | garlic cloves, chopped |
| 1 | (15-ounce) can cannellini beans, rinsed and drained |
| 4 | cups chopped Swiss chard (1 bunch) |
| 6 | cups low-sodium chicken broth |
| 1 | (9-ounce) package cheese tortellini, fresh or frozen |
| ¼ | teaspoon freshly ground black pepper |

In a large, heavy soup pot, heat the olive oil over medium-high heat. Add the pancetta, shallots, carrot, and garlic and cook until the pancetta is crisp, about 5 minutes, stirring occasionally. Add the beans, Swiss chard, and broth.

Bring the soup to a boil over medium-high heat, then reduce the heat to a simmer. Add the tortellini and cook 5 minutes for fresh, 8 minutes for frozen, or until just tender. Season with pepper and serve.

# Pasta e Ceci

## 4 to 6 servings

If you like *pasta e fagioli,* you'll love this rib-sticking soup that substitutes garbanzo beans for the usual cannellinis and adds some tomatoes for color and flavor. It happens to be my Aunt Raffy's favorite soup.

| | |
|---|---|
| 4 | fresh thyme sprigs |
| 1 | large fresh rosemary sprig |
| 1 | bay leaf |
| 1 | tablespoon olive oil |
| 1 | tablespoon unsalted butter |
| 1 | cup chopped onion (1 medium onion) |
| 3 | ounces pancetta, chopped |
| 2 | garlic cloves, minced |
| 6 | cups low-sodium chicken broth |
| 2 | (14.5-ounce) cans garbanzo beans, drained and rinsed |
| 1 | (14.5-ounce) can diced tomatoes, with juice |
| ¾ | cup ditalini (thimble-shaped pasta) |
| ½ | teaspoon salt |
| ½ | teaspoon freshly ground black pepper |
| ⅓ | cup freshly grated Parmesan, for garnish |
| | Extra-virgin olive oil, for drizzling |

Wrap the thyme, rosemary, and bay leaf in a piece of cheesecloth and secure with kitchen twine to make a sachet. Heat the olive oil and butter in a large, heavy saucepan over medium heat. Add the onion, pancetta, and garlic and sauté until the onion is tender, about 3 minutes. Add the broth, beans, tomatoes, and herb sachet. Cover and bring to a boil over medium-high heat, then decrease the heat to medium and simmer until the vegetables are very tender, about 10 minutes. Discard the sachet.

Transfer 1 cup of the bean mixture to a blender and reserve. Add the ditalini to the soup pot, cover, and bring the liquid back to a boil. Boil gently until the pasta is tender but still firm to the bite, about 8 minutes. Purée the reserved bean mixture until smooth, then stir the purée into the boiling soup. Season with salt and freshly ground black pepper.

Ladle the soup into bowls. Sprinkle each serving with some Parmesan and drizzle with extra-virgin olive oil.

# Grating Cheeses

A sprinkling of freshly grated cheese is the finishing touch for many soups as well as pasta dishes, adding a sharp and salty accent. A mellow aged Parmesan is the go-to cheese for most of us, but it's one of many hard cheeses that are suitable for grating, each of which contributes a different dimension to the finished dish. These are the three I use most often; all three melt beautifully without becoming runny or rubbery.

**Asiago:** This aged cow's-milk cheese is made in the Veneto region of Italy and is sold in both a soft, young version and an aged, hard version, which is the one you want for grating. It's aged for a minimum of nine months, and it has a sharp flavor very similar to an aged Cheddar. It's not as buttery as Parmesan, but it can be substituted for it in many recipes, depending on how sharp and robust you like your cheesy topping. I especially like it on hearty dishes with a meat or mushroom sauce.

**Parmigiano-Reggiano:** Considered the finest variety of Parmesan cheese, Parmigiano-Reggiano is a cow's-milk cheese that is aged for up to two years, and its flavor is most pronounced when the cheese is grated. It's slightly salty and fruity with a grainy, brittle texture that is even a bit crunchy; its subtle flavor won't overpower delicate pastas and light cream sauces. Parmigiano-Reggiano is a staple in my fridge, and I use it to enhance the flavor of just about everything, including eggs, veggies, breads, and much more. Authentic Parmigiano-Reggiano is imported from Italy and, although it is pricier than other imported and domestic Parmesans, it is well worth it. Look for the stamp on the rind to make sure you're getting the real thing.

**Pecorino:** Unlike Parmesan, Pecorino is a sheep's-milk cheese (in fact, *pecorino* means "sheep" in Italian). Again, you're looking for the aged hard cheese, not the soft creamy one. Pecorino is aged, but not as long as Parmesan. It has a salty, tangy flavor and it melts beautifully on pasta and sauces. It is a little more assertive than Parmesan and can be substituted for it in many recipes if you want a sharper kick.

# Italian Vegetable Soup

6 servings

You can make this kind of soup anytime, using any kind of pasta you like. Small shapes and short noodles are the obvious choices, but my parents often added spaghetti or fettuccine, broken into small pieces so we could still eat it with a spoon. The fettuccine looks a little more elegant, but if all you have on hand is spaghetti, that's fine; the soup will have a more rustic, homey look.

| | |
|---|---|
| ¼ | cup extra-virgin olive oil |
| 2 | leeks (white and pale green parts only), chopped and well rinsed |
| 4 | garlic cloves, minced |
| 6 | small zucchini, thinly sliced, about 4 cups |
| 2 | (13¾-ounce) cans quartered artichoke hearts packed in water, drained |
| ½ | teaspoon salt |
| ½ | teaspoon freshly ground black pepper |
| 10 | cups vegetable broth |
| 5 | ounces fresh fettuccine, cut into 2- to 3-inch pieces (about 1½ cups) |
| ½ | cup freshly grated Parmesan cheese |
| 3 | tablespoons unsalted butter, softened |
| 2 | tablespoons chopped fresh thyme |

Heat the oil in a large, heavy pot over medium-low heat. Add the leeks and sauté until translucent, about 5 minutes. Add half the minced garlic, the zucchini, artichokes, salt, and pepper, and sauté until the zucchini is tender, about 10 minutes. Add the vegetable broth and simmer, covered, for 20 minutes. Bring the soup back up to a gentle boil over medium-high heat, add the pasta, and cook for 1 minute more (if you are using dried pasta or a different shape, adjust the cooking time accordingly to cook the pasta just to al dente).

Meanwhile, combine the remaining garlic, the Parmesan, softened butter, and thyme in a small bowl and stir with a fork until well blended.

Ladle the soup into bowls. Top with a dollop of the Parmesan mixture and serve.

# Tuscan White Bean and Garlic Soup

4 to 6 servings

I love the velvety texture of this soup. Although it has four cloves of garlic, it's not garlicky because they are poached.

|   |   |
|---|---|
| 2 | tablespoons unsalted butter |
| 1 | tablespoon olive oil |
| 2 | shallots, chopped |
| 1 | fresh sage leaf |
| 2 | (15-ounce) cans cannellini beans, drained and rinsed |
| 4 | cups reduced-sodium chicken broth |
| 4 | garlic cloves, halved |
| 1/2 | cup heavy cream |
| 1/2 | teaspoon freshly ground black pepper |
| 6 | slices ciabatta bread |
|   | Extra-virgin olive oil, for drizzling |

Place a medium, heavy soup pot over medium heat. Add the butter, olive oil, and shallots and cook, stirring occasionally, until the shallots are softened, about 5 minutes. Add the sage and beans and stir to combine. Add the broth and bring the mixture to a simmer. Add the garlic and simmer until the garlic is softened, about 10 minutes. Pour the soup into a large bowl. Carefully ladle one-third to one-half of the soup into a blender and purée until smooth. Be careful to hold the top of the blender tightly, as hot liquids expand when they are blended. Pour the blended soup back into the soup pot. Purée the remaining soup. Once all the soup is blended and back in the soup pot, add the cream and the pepper. Cover and keep warm over very low heat.

Place a grill pan over medium-high heat. Drizzle the ciabatta slices with extra-virgin olive oil. Grill the bread until golden grill marks appear and the bread is warm, about 3 minutes per side. Serve the soup in bowls with the grilled bread alongside.

# Ribollita

4 to 6 servings

Broken strands of spaghetti are the starch in my family's version of ribollita, a thick Tuscan soup that is usually made with cubes of stale bread. We always had odds and ends of long pasta on the pantry shelves when I was a child and serving it this way made a hearty meal out of a little bit of pasta.

| | |
|---|---|
| ¼ | cup extra-virgin olive oil |
| 1 | onion, chopped |
| 1 | carrot, peeled and chopped |
| 4 | ounces pancetta, chopped |
| 2 | garlic cloves, minced |
| ½ | teaspoon salt |
| ½ | teaspoon freshly ground black pepper |
| 1 | tablespoon tomato paste |
| 1 | (14.5-ounce) can diced tomatoes, with juice |
| 1 | (10-ounce) package frozen spinach, thawed and squeezed dry |
| 1 | (15-ounce) can cannellini beans, drained and rinsed |
| 2 | teaspoons herbes de Provence |
| 6 | cups low-sodium chicken broth |
| 1 | bay leaf |
| | 3-inch piece of Parmesan rind |
| 1 | cup spaghetti broken into 1-inch pieces |
| | Grated Parmesan, for serving |

Heat the oil in a large, heavy pot over medium heat. Add the onion, carrot, pancetta, garlic, salt, and pepper. Cook until the onion is golden brown and the pancetta is crisp, stirring occasionally, about 7 minutes. Add the tomato paste and stir until dissolved. Add the tomatoes and stir, scraping the bottom of the pan with a wooden spoon to release all the brown bits. Add the spinach, beans, herbes de Provence, broth, bay leaf, and the Parmesan rind. Bring the soup to a boil, then add the spaghetti, reduce the heat, and simmer for 10 minutes, or until the pasta is al dente.

Discard the Parmesan rind and bay leaf, and ladle the soup into bowls. Sprinkle with Parmesan cheese and serve.

# Tuna, Green Bean, and Orzo Salad

6 servings

Salade Niçoise meets all-American pasta salad in this all-in-one dish that's perfect for a picnic or dinner on a hot summer night. The trick is to use the Italian canned tuna; the flavor of water-packed albacore tuna is just not comparable.

| | |
|---|---|
| 1½ | pounds slender green beans, trimmed and halved crosswise |
| 2 | large red potatoes, diced |
| ½ | pound orzo pasta |
| ⅓ | cup freshly squeezed lemon juice |
| 2 | garlic cloves, finely chopped |
| ⅓ | cup extra-virgin olive oil |
| 1 | teaspoon dried oregano |
| ½ | teaspoon salt |
| ¼ | teaspoon freshly ground black pepper |
| 1 | pint cherry tomatoes, halved |
| ½ | cup chopped fresh basil |
| ¼ | cup chopped fresh flat-leaf parsley |
| 1 | (9-ounce) can Italian oil-packed tuna, drained |

Bring a large pot of salted water to a boil. Add the green beans and cook until crisp-tender, stirring occasionally, about 4 minutes. Using a mesh strainer, transfer the green beans to a large bowl of ice water to cool completely. Drain the green beans and pat dry with a towel. Return the water to a simmer, add the potatoes, and cook until they are just tender but still hold their shape, 8 to 10 minutes. Transfer the potatoes to the ice water to cool completely. Drain the potatoes and pat dry with a towel. Bring the water back to a boil and add the pasta. Cook until tender, stirring occasionally, 10 to 12 minutes. Drain and set aside.

In a small bowl, whisk together the lemon juice, garlic, olive oil, oregano, salt, and pepper. Place the tomatoes, basil, and parsley in a large serving bowl. Add the tuna and toss gently to combine. Add the green beans, potatoes, and pasta. Pour the dressing over the salad and toss again to coat the salad with the dressing.

# Fusilli Salad with Seared Shrimp and Parsley Sauce
4 to 6 servings

Among the many virtues of this salad is that it can be made ahead very successfully and it also looks so attractive.

| | |
|---|---|
| 1 | pound fusilli pasta |
| 1 | pound uncooked large shrimp, peeled and deveined (24 shrimp) |
| 5 | teaspoons olive oil |
| | Salt and freshly ground black pepper |
| ½ | cup low-fat sour cream |
| ½ | cup low-fat yogurt |
| ¼ | cup chopped fresh flat-leaf parsley |
| ¼ | cup chopped fresh chives |
| 2 | tablespoons drained capers |
| 1 | tablespoon freshly squeezed lime juice |
| 1 | teaspoon finely chopped fresh tarragon |
| ½ | teaspoon salt |
| ¼ | teaspoon freshly ground black pepper |
| 2 | heads of Belgian endive, trimmed and leaves separated |

Bring a large pot of salted water to a boil over high heat. Add the pasta and cook until tender, stirring occasionally, 10 to 12 minutes. Drain the pasta and cool.

Toss the shrimp with 2 teaspoons of the oil in a large bowl to coat. Heat the remaining 3 teaspoons of oil in a large, heavy skillet over high heat. Sprinkle with salt and pepper. Sauté the shrimp until they are just cooked through, about 3 minutes. Transfer the shrimp to a plate and cool completely.

In a large bowl, mix together the sour cream, yogurt, parsley, chives, capers, lime juice, tarragon, salt, and pepper. Add the pasta and shrimp and toss to coat.

Arrange the endive leaves around the perimeter of a serving platter, tips out. Spoon the pasta salad into the center of the serving platter. The endive should be peeking out from under the pasta salad. Serve cool or at room temperature.

# Neapolitan Calamari and Shrimp Salad

4 to 6 servings

Men sometimes complain that pasta salads aren't a "real" meal because they're so light. This one will make a believer out of anyone who has turned his nose up at pasta salad in the past. Meaty eggplant chunks, cannellini beans, plus lots of grilled seafood make this as filling and robust as it is attractive on the plate.

| | |
|---|---|
| 4 | cups chicken broth |
| ½ | pound orzo pasta (about 1 cup) |
| ½ | pound calamari, bodies and tentacles |
| ½ | pound large shrimp, peeled and deveined |
| 2 | zucchini, cut lengthwise in 3 slices |
| 1 | Japanese eggplant, cut lengthwise in 3 slices |
| 2 | plum tomatoes, halved lengthwise |
| | Olive oil, for drizzling |
| | Salt |
| | Freshly ground black pepper |
| 1 | (15-ounce) can cannellini beans, drained and rinsed |
| 3 | ounces arugula (about 3 cups) |
| ¾ | cup chopped fresh basil |
| ¼ | cup chopped fresh flat-leaf parsley |
| | Juice of 2 lemons |
| ⅔ | cup extra-virgin olive oil |

Bring the chicken broth to a boil in a large pot over high heat. Add the pasta and cook until tender, stirring occasionally, 10 to 12 minutes. Drain the pasta and place it in a large bowl.

Meanwhile, place a grill pan over medium-high heat or preheat a gas or charcoal grill. Drizzle the seafood, zucchini, eggplant, and tomatoes with olive oil and season with salt and pepper. Grill the calamari and shrimp until just cooked through, 1 to 2 minutes per side. Grill the zucchini and eggplant until tender, about 4 minutes per side. Grill the tomatoes cut side down just until grill marks appear, about 2 minutes.

*(recipe continues)*

Cut the calamari bodies into 1-inch rings. Add the calamari rings and tentacles and the shrimp to the bowl with the orzo. Cut the zucchini, eggplant, and tomatoes into 1-inch pieces and add them to the bowl with the orzo and seafood. Toss to combine. Add the cannellini beans, arugula, basil, parsley, lemon juice, extra-virgin olive oil, 1½ teaspoons salt, and 1½ teaspoons pepper and toss again. Gently spoon the salad into a serving bowl and serve.

# Tips for
# a Perfect Pasta Salad

Cooking pasta for a pasta salad differs in a couple of important ways from cooking pasta that is meant to be served hot. Here are some things to keep in mind:

- Because chilling tends to mute flavors, be sure to salt the water in which you cook the pasta especially generously to really flavor the pasta.

- This is the one time you can cook pasta a bit past al dente; the pasta should be cooked all the way through and soft (but not mushy!), as any uncooked core will be hard and taste starchy.

- Rinse the pasta briefly after draining it to get rid of excess starch, which will make your salad sticky. Again, this is an exception to the general rule!

- Don't dress the salad until right before serving, especially if the dressing contains an acid like vinegar or citrus juice, as it will start to break down the pasta and make it mushy.

# Mediterranean Salad
4 to 6 servings

Couscous is technically a pasta made from semolina, though many people consider it a grain. In southern Italy it is used often, a lasting memento of the Arabs that invaded Sicily in the ninth century. I particularly appreciate the way it cooks so quickly. This is a perfect side dish for large-scale entertaining because it doubles or even triples beautifully.

¼  cup plus 3 tablespoons extra-virgin olive oil
2   garlic cloves, minced
    1-pound box Israeli couscous (or any small pasta)
3   cups reduced-sodium chicken broth
    Juice of 2 lemons
    Zest of 1 lemon
½   teaspoon salt
½   teaspoon freshly ground black pepper
1   cup chopped fresh basil leaves
½   cup chopped fresh mint leaves
¼   cup dried cranberries
¼   cup slivered almonds, toasted (see page 168)

In a medium saucepan, warm the 3 tablespoons of olive oil over medium heat. Add the garlic and cook for 1 minute. Add the couscous and cook until toasted and lightly browned, stirring often, about 5 minutes. Carefully add the broth and the juice of 1 lemon and bring to a boil. Reduce the heat and simmer, covered, until the couscous is tender, stirring occasionally, 10 to 12 minutes. Drain the couscous.

In a large bowl, toss the cooked couscous with the remaining ¼ cup of olive oil, the remaining lemon juice, the zest, salt, and pepper and let cool.

Once the couscous has cooled to room temperature, add the fresh herbs, dried cranberries, and almonds. Toss to combine.

# Antipasto Salad

4 to 6 servings

When we're hosting game night and have lots of my husband's friends coming over, I make this salad. It's hearty and colorful, and because it holds very well at room temperature, I can make it ahead of time so I can take part in game night, too!

### Vinaigrette

| | |
|---|---|
| 1 | bunch of fresh basil, stemmed and chopped (about 2 cups) |
| ¼ | cup red wine vinegar |
| 1 | garlic clove, halved |
| 1 | teaspoon Dijon mustard |
| ½ | teaspoon salt |
| ½ | teaspoon freshly ground black pepper |
| ¾ | cup extra-virgin olive oil |

### Antipasto Salad

| | |
|---|---|
| 1 | pound fusilli pasta |
| ½ | cup hard salami cut into strips (about 3 ounces) |
| ½ | cup smoked turkey cut into strips (about 3 ounces) |
| ¼ | cup Provolone cheese cut into strips |
| ¼ | cup grated Asiago cheese |
| 2 | tablespoons pitted and halved green olives |
| 2 | tablespoons roasted red peppers cut into strips |
| ¼ | teaspoon salt |
| ½ | teaspoon freshly ground black pepper |

In a blender, combine the basil, vinegar, garlic, mustard, salt, and pepper. Blend until the basil and garlic are finely chopped. With the machine running, drizzle in the olive oil until the dressing is smooth.

Bring a large pot of salted water to a boil over high heat. Add the pasta and cook until it's tender, stirring occasionally, 10 to 12 minutes. Drain.

In a large bowl, toss together the cooked pasta with the remaining salad ingredients. Drizzle with the dressing and toss to coat.

# Italian Chicken Salad in Lettuce Cups

## 4 to 6 servings

I rely on this dish whenever I'm hosting a ladies' lunch or wedding shower, or when I just want something tasty and healthy in the refrigerator to snack on. The trick here is using a purchased, roasted whole chicken. It's important to use a whole chicken because it stays moister and more tender than precooked breasts.

| | |
|---|---|
| ½ | cup slivered almonds |
| 1 | pound farfalle pasta |
| 4 | cups coarsely shredded cooked chicken (from about 1½ purchased roasted whole chickens) |
| ½ | cup diced roasted red bell pepper (about 1 pepper) |
| ½ | cup diced roasted yellow bell pepper (about 1 pepper) |
| ½ | red onion, thinly sliced |
| ½ | cup chopped fresh flat-leaf parsley |
| ¼ | cup drained capers |
| ½ | teaspoon salt |
| ¼ | teaspoon freshly ground black pepper |
| 1¼ | cups Red Wine Vinaigrette (page 229) |
| 12 | butter lettuce leaves (from about 2 heads) |
| | 2-ounce chunk of Parmesan cheese, shaved with a vegetable peeler |

Preheat the oven to 350°F. Spread the almonds on a small baking sheet in a single layer. Bake until golden brown, about 10 minutes. Remove from the oven and transfer to a bowl to cool.

Bring a large pot of salted water to a boil over high heat. Add the pasta and cook until tender, stirring occasionally, 10 to 12 minutes. Drain.

In a large bowl, combine the pasta with the chicken, bell peppers, onion, parsley, almonds, capers, salt, and pepper. Drizzle with 1 cup of the vinaigrette and toss gently.

Arrange 1 large lettuce leaf and 1 small lettuce leaf on each plate, overlapping slightly. Spoon the chicken salad into the lettuce "cups." Drizzle the remaining ¼ cup of vinaigrette over the salads. Garnish with shavings of the Parmesan cheese and serve.

# 4

# hearty pastas

When I'm having a hard day, or it's cold and dreary outside, all I crave is a comforting bowl of pasta. There's nothing like a mouthful of creamy, cheesy Venetian "Mac and Cheese" to make me smile and set me up to face a new day. The recipes in this chapter are those I reach for when I need to be warmed from the inside with something that really sticks to the ribs and sustains me. For a lazy winter Sunday I like nothing better than to unwind and make a hearty Sunday dinner; then it's all about a rich, long-cooked ragù and wide, toothsome noodles; the Tagliatelle with Short Rib Ragù cooks for three hours, but the rich, succulent meat is so tender that it falls off the bone, and the wonderful aroma fills your kitchen. You don't need to cook for hours, though, to make this kind of comforting meal; Baked Gnocchi takes almost no time to put together, and the biggest appetites will be satisfied by Rigatoni with Sausage, Peppers, and Onions, or oversized shells stuffed with a mixture of turkey and artichokes. Add a green salad and you've got a perfect winter meal.

# hearty pastas

Baked Penne with Roasted Vegetables

Venetian "Mac and Cheese"

Crab and Ricotta Manicotti

Rigatoni with Sausage, Peppers, and Onions

Roman-Style Fettuccine with Chicken

Farfalle with Creamy Mushroom Gorgonzola Sauce

Pappardelle with Lamb Stew

Cinnamon-Scented Ricotta Ravioli with Beef Ragù

Prosciutto Ravioli

Turkey and Artichoke Stuffed Shells

Gnocchi with Thyme Butter Sauce

Ricotta Gnudi in Parmesan Broth

Tagliatelle with Short Rib Ragù

Penne with Swordfish and Eggplant

Baked Pastina Casserole

Baked Gnocchi

# Baked Penne with Roasted Vegetables
## 6 servings

Here's a great way to get all your veggies in, with tons of flavor. I used to make this often when I was a caterer as an alternative entrée for non-meat eaters because it's an elegant dish with lots of colors and textures. It's also quite convenient, because it can be prepared ahead of time, so if you have vegetarian guests at your next gathering, you can assemble this early and then just pop it in the oven while you're making the rest of the dinner. But don't think this is strictly for vegetarians; it's a real crowd-pleaser all around.

| | |
|---|---|
| 2 | red bell peppers, cored, seeded, and cut into 1-inch strips |
| 2 | zucchini, quartered lengthwise and cut into 1-inch pieces |
| 2 | summer squash, quartered lengthwise and cut into 1-inch pieces |
| 4 | cremini mushrooms, quartered |
| 1 | yellow onion, peeled and sliced into 1-inch strips |
| ¼ | cup extra-virgin olive oil |
| 1 | teaspoon salt |
| ½ | teaspoon freshly ground black pepper |
| 1 | tablespoon dried Italian herb blend or herbes de Provence |
| 1 | pound penne pasta |
| 3 | cups marinara sauce (store-bought or homemade; see page 224) |
| 1 | cup grated fontina cheese |
| ½ | cup grated smoked mozzarella |
| ¼ | cup grated Parmesan, plus ⅓ cup for topping |
| 1½ | cups frozen peas, thawed |
| 2 | tablespoons unsalted butter, cut into small pieces |

Preheat the oven to 450°F.

On a baking sheet, toss the bell peppers, zucchini, squash, mushrooms, and onion with the olive oil, ½ teaspoon of the salt, ¼ teaspoon of the pepper, and the herbs. Bake until tender, about 15 minutes.

Bring a large pot of salted water to a boil over high heat. Add the pasta and cook for about 6 minutes. Since you will be cooking the pasta a second time in the oven, you want to make sure it is not completely cooked. Drain in a colander.

*(recipe continues)*

In a large bowl, combine the pasta with the roasted vegetables, marinara sauce, fontina, mozzarella, ¼ cup of the Parmesan, the peas, and the remaining ½ teaspoon salt and ¼ teaspoon pepper. Gently mix using a wooden spoon until all the pasta is coated with the sauce and the ingredients are combined.

Pour the pasta into a greased 9 x 13 x 2-inch baking dish. Top with the remaining ⅓ cup of Parmesan cheese and the butter pieces. Bake until the top is golden and the cheese melts, about 25 minutes.

## Repurposed Pasta

Many times you don't need an entire pound of pasta to serve your family or guests, but who wants to be left with half-filled boxes of pasta in their pantry? Next time, cook the whole package, use what you need for the meal, and get creative with the leftovers. What can you do with leftover pasta? More than you would imagine:

- Make a pasta frittata by stirring a cup of cooked pasta into beaten, seasoned eggs.
- Deep-fry strands of angel hair or capellini to use as a garnish for soups or salad.
- Dress with a vinaigrette and toss with salad greens.
- Add to soups or plain broths to make them more substantial and satisfying.
- Mix with tomato-based or cream sauce, sprinkle with grated cheese, and bake for a simple impromptu casserole.
- Toss in a skillet with extra-virgin olive oil or butter and garlic to serve as a side dish for grilled meats or fish.

You can also freeze individual portions of pasta for super-fast dinners. Place cooked pasta in a resealable bag with some water and let it cool in the refrigerator, then pop it in the freezer. Just be sure to press as much air as possible from your freezer bags before sealing to prevent freezer burn, and use the frozen pasta within two to three months. Defrost overnight in the refrigerator or dump the frozen pasta directly into boiling water until just heated through.

# Venetian "Mac and Cheese"

6 servings

Although it's not a true-blue, all-American macaroni and cheese because it's made with wide egg noodles rather than the more traditional elbow macaroni or small shell pasta, this is probably the version I make most often. It's a dish I fell in love with when I first had it years ago at Harry's Bar in Venice. Later I re-created it at home as the ultimate comfort food and also to bring back memories of Venice.

|    | Butter for the pan |
|----|--------------------|
| 12 | ounces wide egg noodles |
| 2½ | cups whole milk |
| 2 | cups heavy cream |
| 2 | teaspoons all-purpose flour |
| ½ | teaspoon salt |
| ¼ | teaspoon freshly ground black pepper |
| 2 | cups (packed) grated fontina cheese |
| ¾ | cup (packed) finely grated Parmesan cheese |
| ¾ | cup (packed) grated mozzarella cheese |
| 4 | ounces cooked boiled ham, diced (optional) |
| 2 | tablespoons finely chopped fresh flat-leaf parsley |

Preheat the oven to 450°F. Butter a 9 x 13 x 2-inch glass baking dish. Cook the noodles in a large pot of boiling salted water until tender but still firm to the bite, stirring frequently, about 5 minutes. Drain well (do not rinse).

Whisk the milk, cream, flour, salt, and pepper in a large bowl to blend. Stir in 1 cup of the fontina, ½ cup of the Parmesan, ½ cup of the mozzarella, the ham, and parsley. Add the noodles and toss to coat. Transfer the noodle mixture to the prepared baking dish. Combine the remaining 1 cup of fontina, ¼ cup of Parmesan, and ¼ cup of mozzarella in a small bowl and toss to blend. Sprinkle the cheese mixture over the noodle mixture. Bake until the sauce bubbles and the cheese melts and begins to brown on top, about 15 minutes. Let stand for 10 minutes. Serve warm.

# Crab and Ricotta Manicotti

6 servings

This dish is very elegant, and the combination of crab and creamy béchamel sauce is unusual and delicious. It's a showstopper.

| | |
|---|---|
| 1 | box manicotti pasta (about 12 shells) or an (8-ounce) box cannelloni |
| 1 | cup whole-milk ricotta cheese |
| ¾ | cup grated Parmesan cheese, plus ¼ cup for sprinkling |
| 1 | egg yolk |
| ½ | cup chopped fresh basil |
| 1 | pound lump crabmeat, picked over for shells and cartilage |
| ¼ | teaspoon salt |
| ¼ | teaspoon freshly ground white pepper |
| | Butter for the pan |
| | Béchamel sauce (page 225) |

Bring a large pot of salted water to a boil over high heat. Add the pasta and cook until tender but still firm to the bite, stirring occasionally, 8 to 10 minutes. Drain.

In a large bowl, mix together the ricotta, ¾ cup of the Parmesan, the egg yolk, basil, crab, salt, and pepper.

Preheat the oven to 350°F. Butter a 9 x 13 x 2-inch glass baking dish.

Fill the manicotti with the crab mixture and place in the prepared baking dish. Top the filled manicotti with the béchamel sauce and sprinkle with the remaining ¼ cup of Parmesan cheese. Bake until bubbly and the top is golden brown, 15 to 20 minutes. Serve immediately.

# Rigatoni with Sausage, Peppers, and Onions

4 to 6 servings

Stroll through any Italian-American street fair and you'll smell this classic combo. But while sausage and peppers are great in a sandwich, I think they're even better tossed with rigatoni. Using turkey sausages instead of the more traditional pork also makes it a little lighter.

| | |
|---|---|
| ¼ | cup extra-virgin olive oil |
| 1 | pound sweet Italian turkey sausages |
| 2 | red bell peppers, cored, seeded, and sliced |
| 2 | yellow onions, sliced |
| 1 | teaspoon salt |
| 1 | teaspoon freshly ground black pepper |
| 4 | garlic cloves, chopped |
| ½ | teaspoon dried oregano |
| ½ | cup chopped fresh basil |
| 2 | tablespoons tomato paste |
| 1 | cup Marsala wine |
| 1 | (14.5-ounce) can diced tomatoes, with juice |
| ¼ | teaspoon crushed red pepper flakes (optional) |
| 1 | pound rigatoni pasta |
| | Freshly grated Parmesan cheese, for garnish |

Heat the oil in a large, heavy skillet over medium heat. Add the sausages and cook until brown on all sides, 7 to 10 minutes. Remove the sausages from the pan.

Keeping the pan over medium heat, add the bell peppers, onions, salt, and pepper and cook until golden, 5 minutes. Add the garlic, oregano, and basil and cook for 2 minutes. Add the tomato paste and stir until incorporated, then add the Marsala, tomatoes with their juice, and red pepper flakes, if using. Stir to combine, scraping the bottom of the pan with a wooden spoon to release all the brown bits. Bring to a simmer.

Cut the sausages into 4 to 6 pieces each. Return the sausages to the pan. Simmer uncovered until the sauce has thickened, about 20 minutes.

While the sauce simmers, bring a large pot of salted water to a boil over high heat. Add the pasta and cook until tender but still firm to the bite, stirring occasionally, 8 to 10 minutes. Drain the pasta and add to the thickened sauce; toss to combine. Spoon into individual bowls and sprinkle each serving with Parmesan cheese.

# Roman-Style Fettuccine with Chicken
4 to 6 servings

This is a typically Italian way of preparing chicken, but Italians rarely combine chicken with pasta; by serving chicken over wide ribbons of fettuccine I've created a hybrid Italian-American one-dish meal.

| | |
|---|---|
| ¼ | cup extra-virgin olive oil |
| 4 | boneless, skinless chicken breast halves |
| 2 | boneless, skinless chicken thighs |
| | Salt and freshly ground black pepper |
| 1 | red bell pepper, cored, seeded, and sliced |
| 1 | yellow bell pepper, cored, seeded, and sliced |
| 3 | ounces prosciutto, chopped |
| 2 | garlic cloves, chopped |
| 1 | (14.5-ounce) can diced tomatoes, with juice |
| ½ | cup dry white wine |
| 1 | tablespoon chopped fresh thyme |
| 1 | teaspoon chopped fresh oregano |
| ½ | cup low-sodium chicken broth |
| 1½ | pounds fresh fettuccine |
| 2 | tablespoons drained capers |
| ¼ | cup chopped fresh flat-leaf parsley |

Heat the oil in a large, heavy skillet over medium-high heat. Sprinkle the chicken with salt and pepper. Cook the chicken until brown on both sides, about 4 minutes per side. Remove from the pan and set aside.

Keeping the same pan over medium heat, add the bell peppers and prosciutto and cook until the peppers have browned and the prosciutto is crisp, about 5 minutes. Add the garlic and cook for 1 minute. Add the tomatoes and their juice, wine, thyme, and oregano. Using a wooden spoon, scrape the brown bits off the bottom of the pan. Return the chicken to the pan, add the broth, and bring the mixture to a boil. Reduce the heat, cover, and simmer until the chicken is cooked through, 20 to 30 minutes.

Meanwhile, bring a large pot of salted water to a boil over high heat. Add the fresh pasta, stir, and cook until tender, about 1 minute. Drain.

Remove the chicken and let it cool slightly on a cutting board. Using a fork and knife, gently shred the chicken. Return the chicken to the pan. Stir in the capers and parsley.

To serve, spoon the pasta into serving dishes and top with the chicken and sauce.

# Farfalle with Creamy Mushroom Gorgonzola Sauce

4 to 6 servings

The assertive flavor of Gorgonzola cheese gives the sauce for this dish a nice, sharp bite. This combination of flavors is very typical of northern Italian food, and it makes for a particularly earthy, satisfying dish. You can have fun with this recipe, varying the kinds of mushrooms you use; try to incorporate a few varieties. The frozen peas add a welcome pop of color.

| | |
|---|---|
| 2 | tablespoons unsalted butter |
| 3 | tablespoons all-purpose flour |
| 2½ | cups whole milk, at room temperature |
| 5 | ounces creamy Gorgonzola cheese, cubed |
| | Salt and freshly ground black pepper |
| 3 | tablespoons extra-virgin olive oil |
| 1 | pound assorted mushrooms (such as cremini, oyster, stemmed shiitake), sliced |
| ¾ | cup frozen peas, thawed |
| 1 | pound farfalle pasta |

In a 2-quart saucepan, melt the butter over medium heat. When the butter starts to sizzle, add the flour and whisk until smooth and the flour loses its raw flavor, about 2 minutes. Carefully add the milk all at once and whisk until smooth. Bring the sauce to a simmer. Simmer for 2 minutes, whisking constantly. Remove from the heat. Add the Gorgonzola and stir until melted. Season the sauce to taste with salt and pepper. Set aside and cover to keep warm.

Heat the oil in a large, heavy skillet over medium heat. Add the mushrooms and sauté until tender and golden, about 12 minutes. Stir in the peas. Season the mixture to taste with salt and pepper.

Meanwhile, bring a large pot of salted water to a boil. Add the farfalle and cook until tender but still firm to the bite, stirring often to prevent the pasta from sticking together, about 10 minutes. Drain. Transfer the pasta to a large bowl. Add the Gorgonzola sauce and mushroom mixture, and toss to coat. Season to taste with salt and pepper and serve.

# Pappardelle with Lamb Stew

6 servings

I really prefer the texture of fresh pappardelle with the savory lamb stew; it just seems to absorb the flavors better. If you can't find fresh pappardelle, though, the dried kind is perfectly acceptable, and it's good to have on hand to toss with any leftover braised meats and their braising liquid for a quick, warming meal.

| | |
|---|---|
| 3 | pounds boneless leg of lamb, trimmed of excess fat and sinew, meat cut into 1½- to 2-inch pieces |
| | Salt and freshly ground black pepper |
| 3 | tablespoons all-purpose flour |
| ¼ | cup extra-virgin olive oil |
| 3 | garlic cloves, finely chopped |
| 1½ | cups dry red wine |
| 3½ | cups beef broth |
| 1 | (14.5-ounce) can diced tomatoes, with juice |
| 1 | tablespoon tomato paste |
| 18 | small cipolline onions |
| 2 | large carrots, peeled, cut into 1-inch pieces |
| 1½ | pounds pappardelle pasta, preferably fresh |
| 2 | tablespoons unsalted butter |
| ¼ | cup freshly grated Parmesan cheese |
| ¼ | cup finely chopped fresh flat-leaf parsley |

Sprinkle the lamb with salt and pepper. Toss the lamb with the flour in a large bowl to coat. Heat the oil in a heavy, large pot over medium-high heat. Working in 2 or 3 batches, add the lamb to the pot and cook until brown on all sides, about 10 minutes. Transfer the lamb to a bowl. Add the garlic to the same pot and sauté over medium heat until tender and fragrant, about 1 minute. Add the wine and simmer over medium-high heat until reduced by half, stirring to scrape up any browned bits on the bottom of the pot. Return the lamb to the pot and stir in the broth, tomatoes with their juice, and tomato paste. Cover partially and simmer over medium-low heat, stirring occasionally.

While the stew simmers, cook the onions in a medium saucepan of boiling water for 2 minutes. Drain and cool. Peel the onions and cut off the root ends. When the stew has cooked for 1 hour, add the onions and carrots. Simmer, uncovered, until the lamb and vegetables are tender, about 25 minutes longer. Season the stew with salt and pepper.

Bring a large pot of salted water to a boil over high heat. Add the pasta, stir, and cook until tender, about 1 minute. Drain the pasta and toss with the butter and Parmesan.

Spoon the stew over the pasta, and top with a sprinkle of chopped parsley.

# Cinnamon-Scented Ricotta Ravioli with Beef Ragù

4 to 6 servings

Using cinnamon to flavor a beef dish may sound strange to anyone who is not familiar with the cuisine of southern Italy, where the Moorish influence is apparent in the seasonings of many dishes. I promise, though, the spice is a fantastic addition. The cinnamon gives the sauce a little sweetness and a little heat all in one without being spicy, per se. Try it.

### Cinnamon-Scented Ravioli

| | |
|---|---|
| 2 | (15-ounce) containers whole-milk ricotta cheese |
| ¼ | cup chopped fresh basil |
| ½ | teaspoon ground cinnamon |
| ½ | teaspoon salt |
| ¼ | teaspoon freshly grated nutmeg |
| ¼ | teaspoon freshly ground black pepper |
| 1 | egg, lightly beaten |
| 72 | small square wonton wrappers |

### Beef Ragù

| | |
|---|---|
| 3 | tablespoons olive oil |
| 1 | pound ground beef |
| 1 | carrot, peeled and chopped |
| 1 | medium onion, chopped |
| 2 | garlic cloves, minced |
| ½ | teaspoon salt |
| ½ | teaspoon freshly ground black pepper |
| 2 | tablespoons tomato paste |
| ¾ | cup dry red wine |
| 3½ | cups marinara sauce (store-bought or homemade; see page 224) |
| 3 | tablespoons extra-virgin olive oil, for serving |
| ¼ | cup freshly grated Parmesan cheese, for serving |

To make the ravioli: Combine the ricotta, basil, cinnamon, salt, nutmeg, pepper, and egg in a large mixing bowl. Stir to combine. Place 8 to 10 wonton squares on a dry work surface. Spoon 1 tablespoon of the ricotta mixture into the middle of each square. Dip a pastry brush in a bit of water and wet the square around the ricotta mixture. Place another square

over the filling. Carefully smooth out all the air bubbles and press firmly around the ricotta mixture to create a seal. Use a 2¾-inch square cookie cutter or a 3-inch round cookie cutter to cut out a ravioli. Place the ravioli on a dry baking sheet and continue with another batch of ravioli. The mixture should make about 36 ravioli.

To make the beef ragù: Heat the olive oil in a large, heavy skillet over medium heat. Add the ground beef and cook until it is starting to brown, about 5 minutes. Add the carrot, onion, and garlic. Continue cooking to brown the onion and carrot, about 4 minutes. Add the salt, pepper, tomato paste, and red wine. Use a wooden spoon to scrape the brown bits off the bottom of the pan and dissolve the tomato paste. Continue cooking until the wine is almost completely evaporated. Add the marinara sauce and bring to a simmer. Cover and cook for 10 minutes over low heat.

Bring a large pot of salted water to a boil over high heat. Add the ravioli in batches, being careful not to overcrowd the pot. Cook, stirring occasionally, until the ravioli float, 2 to 3 minutes. Remove the ravioli using a slotted spoon and place on individual plates, or a large serving platter, that have been drizzled with extra-virgin olive oil. Spoon the beef ragù over the ravioli. Sprinkle with Parmesan cheese. Serve immediately.

# Prosciutto Ravioli

6 servings

This is a variation on the ricotta and spinach ravioli recipe from my first book, *Everyday Italian*. The original is one of my very favorite dishes, but my husband, Todd, never feels completely satisfied with a meatless meal so I came up with this version for him. The prosciutto adds body and a kick of flavor to the ravioli, making it a more substantial, manly dish.

| | |
|---|---|
| 1 | (15-ounce) container whole-milk ricotta cheese |
| 1 | (10-ounce) package frozen chopped spinach, thawed, squeezed dry |
| 4 | ounces thinly sliced prosciutto, chopped |
| 2 | large egg yolks |
| 3/4 | teaspoon salt |
| 1/2 | teaspoon freshly ground black pepper |
| 48 | square wonton wrappers |
| 1/2 | cup (1 stick) unsalted butter |
| 1 1/2 | teaspoons dried oregano |
| | Freshly grated Pecorino cheese |

Whisk the ricotta, spinach, prosciutto, egg yolks, salt, and pepper in a medium bowl to blend.

Place 1 tablespoon of the ricotta filling in the center of a wonton wrapper. Brush the edge of the wrapper lightly with water. Fold the wrapper in half point to point, enclosing the filling completely and forming a triangle. Pinch the edges to seal. Transfer the ravioli to a baking sheet. Repeat with the remaining filling and wrappers. (The ravioli can be prepared up to 2 hours ahead; cover and refrigerate.)

Bring a large pot of salted water to a boil. Working in batches, cook the ravioli until just tender, stirring occasionally, about 4 minutes per batch. Transfer the ravioli to a large shallow bowl.

Melt the butter in a small, heavy skillet over medium heat. Add the oregano and stir for 1 minute. Season to taste with salt and pepper. Pour the oregano butter over the ravioli and toss gently to coat. Sprinkle with the Pecorino cheese and serve.

# Turkey and Artichoke Stuffed Shells

6 to 8 servings

Todd and I both love stuffed shells, so I'm always thinking of fun new fillings to try. This one is a real home run. The first time I made it I used leftover dark meat from our Thanksgiving turkey and chopped it fine, but we liked it so much that I've adapted the recipe for ground raw turkey. Now we can have it any night of the year! We like it with the slightly spicy arrabbiata sauce, because turkey can be a bit on the bland side (especially if you can only get ground white-meat turkey), but if you want to use your favorite jarred marinara sauce instead, it's still a great dish.

| | |
|---|---|
| 1 | (12-ounce) box jumbo pasta shells |
| 3 | tablespoons extra-virgin olive oil |
| $\frac{1}{2}$ | large yellow onion, chopped (about 1 cup) |
| 3 | garlic cloves, chopped |
| 1 | pound ground turkey, preferably dark meat or a mix of dark and light meats |
| | Salt and freshly ground black pepper |
| 1 | (8- to 10-ounce) package frozen artichokes, thawed and coarsely chopped |
| 1 | (15-ounce) container whole-milk ricotta cheese |
| $\frac{3}{4}$ | cup freshly grated Parmesan cheese |
| 2 | eggs, lightly beaten |
| $\frac{1}{4}$ | cup chopped fresh basil |
| 2 | tablespoons chopped fresh flat-leaf parsley |
| 5 | cups Arrabbiata Sauce (page 225) or marinara sauce (store-bought or homemade, see page 224) |
| $1\frac{1}{2}$ | cups grated mozzarella cheese (about 5 ounces) |

Preheat the oven to 350°F.

Bring a large pot of salted water to a boil over high heat. Add the pasta and partially cook until tender but still very firm to the bite, stirring occasionally, 4 to 5 minutes. Drain.

Meanwhile, in a large, heavy skillet, heat the olive oil over medium-high heat. Add the onion and the garlic and cook until the onion is soft and starting to brown, about 3 minutes. Add

*(recipe continues)*

the ground turkey, ½ teaspoon salt, and ¼ teaspoon pepper and continue to cook, stirring occasionally, until the meat is lightly golden and cooked through. Add the artichoke hearts and stir to combine. Remove from the heat and let cool.

In a large bowl, combine the cooled turkey mixture with the ricotta cheese, Parmesan cheese, eggs, basil, parsley, ½ teaspoon salt, and ½ teaspoon pepper. Stir to combine.

Cover the bottom of a 9 x 13 x 2-inch baking dish with 1 cup of the Arrabbiata Sauce. Hold a shell in the palm of your hand and stuff it with a large spoonful of turkey mixture, about 2 tablespoons. Place the stuffed shell in the baking dish. Continue filling the shells until the baking dish is full; you should have about 24 shells. Drizzle the remaining Arrabbiata Sauce over the shells and top with the grated mozzarella. Bake until the shells are warmed through and the cheese is beginning to brown, about 25 minutes.

# Gnocchi with Thyme Butter Sauce

4 to 6 servings (makes about 54 gnocchi)

I happen to love gnocchi; they're like little pillows in your mouth, and very, very comforting. Although you can get them at any grocery store these days, when I have some time, I still enjoy making them at home.

Gnocchi

2    baking potatoes, such as russets (about 12 ounces each)
1    egg, lightly beaten
1    teaspoon salt
½    teaspoon freshly ground black pepper
¾    cup all-purpose flour
¼    cup shaved Pecorino Romano, for garnish

Thyme Butter Sauce

¾    cup unsalted butter (1½ sticks)
1    tablespoon fresh thyme leaves
     Salt and freshly ground black pepper

To make the gnocchi, pierce the potatoes all over with a fork. Microwave the potatoes on High until tender, turning once, about 12 minutes. (You can also bake the potatoes at 375°F for 50 minutes, or until tender.) While the potatoes are still warm, cut them in half and scoop the flesh into a large bowl. Discard the skin. Using a fork, mash the potato well. Stir in the egg, salt, and pepper. Sift the flour over the potato mixture and stir just until blended.

Scoop out a large spoonful of gnocchi dough. Roll each scoop on the work surface into about a ½-inch-diameter rope. Cut the dough into 1-inch pieces. Roll each piece of dough over a wooden paddle with ridges or over the tines of a fork to form grooves in the dough. Set the formed gnocchi on a baking sheet while you form the rest of the dough.

To make the thyme butter, melt the butter with the thyme leaves in a medium, heavy skillet over medium heat until the butter is melted, about 2 minutes.

Working in two batches, cook the gnocchi in a large pot of boiling salted water until they have all risen to the surface, about 3 minutes. Scoop the gnocchi into a colander with a slotted spoon while you cook the second batch. Reheat the thyme butter sauce over low heat. Transfer the cooked gnocchi to the skillet with the hot thyme butter and toss to coat. Sprinkle with salt and freshly ground black pepper and toss again.

Spoon the gnocchi and butter sauce into shallow bowls. Top with the Pecorino and serve.

# Ricotta Gnudi in Parmesan Broth

4 to 6 servings

*Gnudi* translates literally as "nude," a reference to the fact that these little dumplings are basically "naked" raviolis—the fillings without their pasta wrappers. Served in a savory broth, this is a comforting winter meal.

### Parmesan Broth

| | |
|---|---|
| 6 | cups low-sodium chicken broth |
| 1 | teaspoon freshly ground black pepper |
| ¼ | cup freshly grated Parmesan cheese |

### Ricotta Gnudi

| | |
|---|---|
| 2½ | cups whole-milk ricotta cheese |
| ½ | cup freshly grated Parmesan cheese |
| 1 | egg |
| 1 | egg white |
| 2 | ounces prosciutto, chopped |
| 2 | tablespoons chopped fresh flat-leaf parsley |
| ¼ | teaspoon freshly grated nutmeg |
| 1 | teaspoon salt |
| ½ | teaspoon freshly ground black pepper |
| ½ | cup plus 2 tablespoons all-purpose flour, plus 1 cup for dredging |

Bring the chicken broth to a boil in a medium saucepan over high heat. Reduce the heat to medium-low and simmer until the broth has reduced to 4 cups, about 20 minutes.

Meanwhile, make the gnudi. Bring a large pot of salted water to a simmer over high heat. In a large bowl, combine the ricotta, Parmesan, egg, egg white, prosciutto, parsley, nutmeg, salt, and pepper and mix thoroughly. When the water is simmering and ready, stir the flour into the ricotta mixture. (It is important not to add the flour too soon; otherwise they will become dense and gummy, not light.) Shape the gnudi using two large soup spoons: scoop up a large spoonful of ricotta mixture into one spoon, then scoop the mixture onto the other spoon and back again, forming a three-sided oval. Drop the gnudi into the dredging flour. Form another 8 or 9 gnudi at a time, dredge in flour on all sides, and tap off the excess.

Slide the formed gnudi into the simmering water, being careful not to overcrowd the pot. Remove the gnudi using a slotted spoon after they have floated to the top and have cooked for about 4 minutes total. While the gnudi cook, create another batch of gnudi and dredge them in flour. Continue cooking and forming gnudi, transferring the cooked gnudi to a platter in a single layer, until you have used all the ricotta mixture.

Divide the gnudi among the serving bowls. Pour the reduced broth over the gnudi. Sprinkle with a pinch of the pepper and a spoonful of grated Parmesan and serve.

# Tagliatelle with Short Rib Ragù
## 4 to 6 servings

Although this dish takes almost three hours to make, I promise you it's *so* worth it. The short ribs become incredibly tender and moist, they fall off the bone. It's the kind of meal you will dream about on a snowy night. The twist here is the shaved bittersweet chocolate, which gives the dish a sweet and savory yet extremely subtle component. You can leave it out, but trust me when I tell you that it's the element everyone will be talking about when they taste this.

| | |
|---|---|
| 3 | tablespoons olive oil |
| 2 | ounces pancetta, chopped (about ½ cup) |
| 2½ | pounds short ribs |
| | Salt and freshly ground black pepper |
| ¼ | cup all-purpose flour |
| 1 | medium onion, chopped |
| 1 | carrot, peeled and chopped |
| ½ | cup fresh flat-leaf parsley leaves |
| 2 | garlic cloves |
| 1 | (14.5-ounce) can tomatoes (whole or diced) |
| 1 | tablespoon tomato paste |
| 1 | teaspoon chopped fresh rosemary |
| 1 | teaspoon dried thyme |
| ½ | teaspoon dried oregano |
| 1 | bay leaf |
| 2½ | cups beef broth |
| ¾ | cup red wine |
| 1 | pound fresh or dried tagliatelle |
| 4 | to 6 teaspoons shaved bittersweet chocolate |

Heat the olive oil in a large, heavy soup pot over medium heat. Cook the pancetta until golden and crisp, about 4 minutes. Meanwhile, season the short ribs with salt and pepper, and dredge in the flour. Using a slotted spoon, remove the pancetta from the pan and set it aside. Add the short ribs to the pan and cook until browned on all sides, about 7 minutes total. Meanwhile, combine the onion, carrot, parsley, garlic, tomatoes, and tomato paste in

*(recipe continues)*

a food processor and pulse until finely minced. Once the short ribs are browned, add the minced vegetables to the pot along with the pancetta and stir. Add the rosemary, thyme, oregano, bay leaf, beef broth, and wine. Bring the mixture to a boil, then reduce the heat, cover, and simmer for 1 hour and 15 minutes. Remove the lid and simmer for another hour and 30 minutes, stirring occasionally. Using a slotted spoon, lift out the short ribs and let cool briefly on a plate. Shred the meat and return it to the pot, discarding the bones. Discard the bay leaf. Add ½ teaspoon salt and ¾ teaspoon pepper.

Bring a large pot of salted water to a boil over high heat. Add the pasta and cook until tender but still firm to the bite, stirring occasionally, 8 to 10 minutes for dried pasta or 2 to 3 minutes for fresh. Drain the pasta, reserving 1 cup of the cooking liquid. Add the pasta to the pot with the short rib ragù and stir to combine. If needed, add the reserved pasta liquid ¼ cup at a time to moisten the pasta. Transfer to serving bowls, top each bowl with 1 teaspoon of chocolate shavings, and serve immediately.

# Penne with Swordfish and Eggplant

4 to 6 servings

Many Sicilian dishes feature swordfish, since it is very plentiful in the waters surrounding the island. Eggplant is also found in many dishes from this area, but I prefer the texture and taste of Japanese eggplants over the larger ones because their seeds are so tiny; there is also no need to salt the cubed eggplant because they aren't as bitter as the fully mature ones can be.

| | |
|---|---|
| 1 | pound penne rigata |
| ⅓ | cup plus 2 tablespoons olive oil |
| 3 | garlic cloves, minced |
| ½ | teaspoon crushed red pepper flakes, plus more to taste |
| ¼ | cup plus ⅓ cup chopped fresh flat-leaf parsley |
| 4 | Japanese eggplants, ends trimmed, cut into thirds lengthwise, then cut into 1-inch pieces |
| 1 | pound swordfish steaks, skin removed, cut into 1-inch cubes |
| | Salt and freshly ground black pepper |
| ⅓ | cup dry white wine |
| 2 | cups halved teardrop or cherry tomatoes (red, yellow, or a blend) |
| | Extra-virgin olive oil, for drizzling |

Bring a large pot of salted water to a boil over high heat. Add the pasta and cook until tender but still firm to the bite, stirring occasionally, 8 to 10 minutes. Drain.

Meanwhile, place a large, heavy skillet over medium-high heat. Add the ⅓ cup olive oil, the garlic, red pepper flakes, and the ¼ cup parsley. Stir and cook until fragrant, 1 or 2 minutes. Add the eggplant and cook until tender, about 5 minutes. Use a slotted spoon to remove the eggplant from the pan and set aside. Season the swordfish cubes with salt and pepper.

Add the remaining 2 tablespoons of olive oil to the same pan, and cook the swordfish over medium-high heat until opaque, about 5 minutes, turning with a rubber spatula once or twice. Add the white wine and cook until almost evaporated, about 2 minutes. Turn off the heat. Add the tomatoes, eggplant, drained pasta, and the remaining ⅓ cup of parsley and stir. Drizzle with extra-virgin olive oil and sprinkle with more salt and pepper to taste. Stir to combine and serve.

# Baked Pastina Casserole

## 4 servings

I've made this with lots of different pasta shapes—little stars, tiny elbows, ditalini, tiny wagon wheels—so use whichever you like or have on hand. In a pinch, you can even break a handful of spaghetti into small pieces if you don't have any short-cut pasta on the shelf. It's a perfect portable dish, a nice choice if you want to make something to take to a party or a new neighbor.

| | |
|---|---|
| 1 | cup pastina (or any small pasta) |
| 2 | tablespoons olive oil |
| ½ | cup cubed chicken breast (1-inch cubes) |
| ½ | cup diced onion (about ½ small onion) |
| 1 | garlic clove, minced |
| 1 | (14.5-ounce) can diced tomatoes, with juice |
| 1 | cup shredded mozzarella |
| ¼ | cup chopped fresh flat-leaf parsley |
| ¼ | teaspoon salt |
| ¼ | teaspoon freshly ground black pepper |
| ¼ | cup bread crumbs |
| ¼ | cup freshly grated Parmesan cheese |
| 1 | tablespoon unsalted butter, cut in small pieces, plus more for buttering the baking dish |

Preheat the oven to 400°F.

Bring a medium pot of salted water to a boil over high heat. Add the pasta and cook until just tender, stirring occasionally, about 5 minutes. Drain the pasta and transfer to a large mixing bowl.

Meanwhile, heat the olive oil in a medium sauté pan over medium heat. Add the chicken and cook for 3 minutes. Add the onion and garlic, stirring to combine, and cook until the onion is soft and the chicken is cooked through, about 5 minutes more. Add the chicken mixture to the bowl with the drained pasta, then add the canned tomatoes and their juice, mozzarella cheese, parsley, salt, and pepper. Stir to combine.

Butter an 8 x 8 x 2-inch baking dish and spread the pasta in the prepared dish. In a small bowl, mix together the bread crumbs and the Parmesan cheese. Sprinkle over the top of the pasta. Dot the top with small bits of butter. Bake until the top is golden brown, about 30 minutes.

# Baked Gnocchi
## 6 servings

For this dish, be sure to use the vacuum-packed type of gnocchi, not those that come hard and dry in a box, as they are full of preservatives. You can also buy fresh gnocchi at many specialty food shops, or even make your own (see page 109), though that's not really necessary for this dish. It's a little spin on the basic gnocchi dish that's also a really colorful meal-in-one, packed with spinach and cheese.

| | |
|---|---|
| 2 | (17-ounce) packages potato gnocchi |
| 3 | cups heavy cream |
| 1 | cup reduced-sodium chicken broth |
| ¼ | cup all-purpose flour |
| ½ | teaspoon salt |
| ½ | teaspoon freshly ground black pepper |
| ¼ | teaspoon freshly grated nutmeg |
| 12 | ounces baby spinach |
| 3 | ounces fresh goat cheese |
| ½ | cup freshly grated Parmesan cheese |

Preheat the oven to 400°F.

Place the gnocchi in a lightly greased 9 x 13 x 2-inch baking dish. Set aside.

In a medium saucepan, whisk together the cream, chicken broth, and flour over medium heat. Continue whisking until the sauce is simmering and thickened, about 5 minutes. Add the salt, pepper, and nutmeg and stir to combine. Add the spinach and toss to coat in the cream. Pour the cream and spinach mixture evenly over the gnocchi and gently spread the spinach out to cover.

Crumble the goat cheese over the spinach. Sprinkle with the Parmesan cheese. Bake until the top is golden in places, about 30 minutes.

# 5

# on the lighter side

People are always asking how I can cook the way I do and not gain weight. The truth is that if I ate fettuccine carbonara or a big plate of baked manicotti every night, I probably would; fortunately, so many of my favorite pastas are light, filled with vegetables and loaded with flavor. These are the recipes I turn to in the summer months, when the farmer's market is loaded with beautiful produce that needs very little beyond a sprinkle of fresh herbs, a little grated cheese, and some freshly cooked pasta to make a completely delicious meal. Linguine with Butter, Pecorino, Arugula, and Black Pepper is probably the fastest pasta dish you can make, but it is full-flavored and delicious, with a nice, peppery kick from the arugula, cheese, and freshly ground pepper. I particularly like to pair pasta with fish and seafood because they both cook so quickly and their light textures don't weigh me down. If you're looking for fast and fresh, you'll find a treasure trove of recipes here.

# on the lighter side

Linguine with Butter, Pecorino, Arugula, and Black Pepper

Saffron Orzo with Shrimp

Penne with Spicy Tomato Sauce

Spaghetti with Sautéed Onions and Marjoram

Eggplant Mezzaluna Ravioli

Orecchiette with Mixed Greens and Goat Cheese

Capellini Piedmontese

Spaghetti alla Pirata

Spaghetti with Red and Yellow Peppers

Swordfish and Spaghetti with Citrus Pesto

Conghilie with Clams, Mussels, and Broccoli

Rotini with Salmon and Roasted Garlic

Rigatoni with Red Pepper, Almonds, and Bread Crumbs

Angel Hair Pasta with Sun-Dried Tomatoes and
Goat Cheese

# Linguine with Butter, Pecorino, Arugula, and Black Pepper

6 servings

Simple, simple, simple, but so good—this is truly one of the fastest dishes you can make, and one of the best.

| | |
|---|---|
| 1 | pound linguine |
| ¼ | cup (½ stick) unsalted butter, at room temperature |
| 1¼ | cups very finely grated Pecorino Romano cheese |
| 1½ | teaspoons freshly ground black pepper |
| 1 | cup coarsely chopped arugula |
| | Salt, to taste |

Bring a large pot of salted water to a boil over high heat. Add the linguine and cook until it is al dente, stirring frequently, about 8 minutes. Drain, reserving 1½ cups of the pasta water.

Immediately toss the hot pasta in a large bowl with the butter to coat. While tossing the linguine, gradually sprinkle the cheese, pepper, and enough of the reserved pasta water evenly over the linguine to moisten. Add the arugula and toss to combine. Season the pasta with salt. Divide the pasta among 6 plates and serve.

# No-Cook Pasta Sauces

When it's hot outside, the idea of turning on the stove to do more than boil water for pasta is just not appealing. On days like those I like to toss cooked pasta with a fresh sauce that requires no cooking at all! You can use raw or leftover cooked or roasted vegetables, herbs, cheese, even bits of cooked meat; just make sure there is enough liquid to moisten the pasta, whether it's oil, juice, broth, or a splash of the pasta cooking water. Here are some of my favorite "raw" sauces:

• Toss the ingredients of a caprese salad (fresh mozzarella, tomatoes, basil, a little chopped garlic, extra-virgin olive oil, and salt and pepper) with cooked pasta in any shape or size, and voilà! Dinner is ready.

• Whisk together lemon juice, lemon zest, grated Parmesan, extra-virgin olive oil, and salt and pepper in a serving bowl. Add freshly cooked capellini and toss.

• Combine chopped kalamata olives, capers, chopped arugula, extra-virgin olive oil, and salt and pepper in a bowl. Toss well with cooked pasta and sprinkle with grated Pecorino cheese.

• I love the convenience of rotisserie chickens. I like to shred the meat and toss it with cooked pasta, some chicken broth, and a bit of pasta water, extra-virgin olive oil, salt and pepper, some toasted pine nuts, and Parmesan cheese for a quick weeknight meal. Add spinach or arugula leaves for color.

• For the simplest, quickest pasta meal, combine small bits of butter, grated Parmesan, and chopped herbs like parsley or basil in a bowl with hot cooked pasta; it is comforting and super easy.

# Saffron Orzo with Shrimp

6 servings

What began as a simple side dish with a citrusy dressing became a light but appealing entrée with the addition of quickly sautéed shrimp. This can be served warm, but it's also nice at room temperature, making it a good option for picnics or buffet spreads.

| | |
|---|---|
| 4 | cups reduced-sodium chicken broth |
| 1 | teaspoon saffron threads |
| 1 | pound orzo (small, rice-shaped pasta) |
| 7 | tablespoons extra-virgin olive oil |
| ¼ | cup chopped fresh flat-leaf parsley |
| | Juice of 1 lemon |
| 3 | teaspoons salt |
| 2 | teaspoons freshly ground black pepper |
| 1 | pound large shrimp, peeled and deveined |

In a large pot, bring the chicken broth to a boil over high heat. Reduce the heat to low, bringing the broth to a simmer. Add the saffron, stir, and simmer until the saffron has "bloomed," about 5 minutes. Return the heat to medium and bring the stock to a boil, then add the orzo and cook until tender but still firm to the bite, stirring occasionally, 8 to 10 minutes. Drain the orzo and transfer to a large bowl. Add 4 tablespoons of olive oil, the parsley, half the lemon juice, 2 teaspoons salt, and 1 teaspoon pepper and combine thoroughly.

In a bowl, toss the shrimp with 1 teaspoon salt, 1 teaspoon pepper, and the remaining lemon juice. Heat the remaining 3 tablespoons of olive oil in a medium skillet over medium-high heat. Add the shrimp in a single layer and cook until the shrimp are just turning pink, about 2 minutes per side. Add the shrimp to the bowl with the orzo. Toss to combine and serve.

# Penne with Spicy Tomato Sauce

4 to 6 servings

Somewhat reminiscent of a puttanesca sauce, but with the addition of olives and lots of vegetables, this is a homey dish that you would find in many Roman kitchens. Long, slow simmering is what makes the sauce so delicious, so if you like, make a double batch and freeze some to use next time you bake fish or chicken, or make a baked pasta dish.

| | |
|---|---|
| ¼ | cup extra-virgin olive oil |
| 1 | small onion, finely chopped |
| 1 | garlic clove, finely chopped |
| 1 | celery stalk, finely chopped |
| 1 | carrot, peeled and finely chopped |
| ¼ | teaspoon salt, plus more to taste |
| ½ | teaspoon freshly ground black pepper, plus more to taste |
| 1 | (28-ounce) can crushed tomatoes, with juice |
| 1 | dried bay leaf |
| 8 | anchovy fillets packed in olive oil, minced |
| ¾ | cup pitted kalamata olives, halved |
| 2 | tablespoons drained capers |
| 1 | teaspoon crushed red pepper flakes |
| 1 | pound penne pasta |
| 3 | tablespoons chopped fresh flat-leaf parsley |

In a large casserole or Dutch oven, heat the oil over medium heat. Add the onion and garlic and sauté until translucent, about 10 minutes. Add the celery, carrot, and ¼ teaspoon each of salt and pepper. Sauté until all the vegetables are soft, about 10 minutes longer. Add the tomatoes and bay leaf, and simmer uncovered over low heat until the sauce thickens, stirring occasionally, about 1 hour. Add 1 cup of water if the sauce gets too thick. Remove and discard the bay leaf.

Place the minced anchovies and some of their oil in a medium, heavy skillet. Stir over medium heat until the anchovies melt, about 2 minutes. Add the olives, capers, remaining ¼ teaspoon pepper, and red pepper flakes. Sauté until the olives are heated through, about 2 minutes. Stir the olive mixture into the sauce and simmer over medium heat until the flavors blend, stirring frequently, about 5 minutes. Season with more salt to taste.

Meanwhile, bring a large pot of salted water to a boil. Add the penne and cook until tender but still firm to the bite, stirring often to prevent the pasta from sticking together, about 10 minutes. Drain, reserving 1 cup of the pasta water. Add the penne to the sauce and toss to coat, adding enough of the reserved pasta water to moisten. Transfer the pasta to a large serving bowl. Sprinkle with the parsley and serve.

# Spaghetti with Sautéed Onions and Marjoram

4 to 6 servings

Meyer lemons are sweeter than regular lemons and, unfortunately, are in season for only a short time each year. Since they are hard to find, I've fallen in love with Meyer lemon olive oil, which captures their flavor very well and adds both citrus tang and a hint of sweetness to all kinds of recipes. Because this is such a simple dish—the sauce is just onions, the oil, and fresh marjoram—do try to get your hands on some Meyer lemon olive oil; I use the one made by DaVero. If you can't find it, though, you can use the citrus oil on page 226.

| | |
|---|---|
| 1 | pound spaghetti |
| ¼ | cup Meyer lemon olive oil or Citrus Olive Oil (page 226) |
| 2 | large red onions, cut into ¼-inch-thick rings |
| 2 | teaspoons chopped fresh marjoram |
| 8 | ounces feta cheese, cubed |
| | Sea salt and freshly ground black pepper |

Bring a large pot of salted water to a boil. Add the spaghetti and cook until tender but still firm to the bite, stirring occasionally, about 8 minutes. Drain, reserving 1 cup of the pasta water.

Meanwhile, heat 2 tablespoons of the oil in a large, heavy skillet over medium heat. Add the onions and sauté until tender and beginning to brown, about 15 minutes. Stir in the marjoram and sauté until fragrant, about 1 minute. Add the cooked pasta and the remaining 2 tablespoons of oil and toss with ¼ cup of the reserved pasta water at a time until moistened. Add the feta cheese and toss again, then season the pasta with salt and pepper to taste. Transfer to bowls and serve.

# Eggplant Mezzaluna Ravioli

4 to 6 servings

Ravioli are a slam dunk with most people, and making them in the half-moon, or *mezzaluna,* shape makes a classic preparation a little more elegant. Between the oregano, the fontina cheese, and the meaty eggplant, the filling is quite hearty so I dress these simply with a little extra-virgin olive oil and fresh herbs.

| | |
|---|---|
| ⅓ | cup olive oil |
| ½ | large onion, diced |
| 1 | large eggplant (about 1½ to 2 pounds), diced |
| 2 | garlic cloves, minced |
| ½ | teaspoon chopped fresh oregano, plus 1 teaspoon fresh oregano leaves, for garnish |
| ½ | cup grated fontina cheese (about 2 ounces) |
| ½ | cup whole-milk ricotta cheese |
| ½ | teaspoon salt, plus more for sprinkling |
| ¼ | teaspoon freshly ground black pepper, plus more for sprinkling |
| 1 | package square wonton wrappers (about 50 to 60 wrappers) |
| ¼ | to ½ cup extra-virgin olive oil, for garnish |

Heat the olive oil in a large, heavy skillet over medium heat. Add the onion and cook until tender, about 3 minutes. Add the eggplant, garlic, and chopped oregano, and continue to cook until the eggplant is soft and starting to fall apart, about 12 minutes. Transfer the eggplant mixture to a medium bowl and let cool.

Once the eggplant mixture is cool, add the cheeses, salt, and pepper. Place 6 wonton squares on a dry work surface. Place 1 teaspoon of the eggplant mixture on each square. Dip a pastry brush in water and wet around the edges of the square. Fold the square in half to form a rectangle. Using a 3-inch-diameter scalloped-edged cookie cutter, press around the filling to make a half-moon shape. Place the finished ravioli on a dry baking sheet. Continue with the remaining filling. You should be able to make about 60 ravioli.

Bring a large pot of salted water to a boil over high heat. Add the ravioli (you may want to cook them in two batches) and cook until heated through, stirring occasionally, about 2 minutes. Drain the ravioli. Drizzle a small amount of extra-virgin olive oil on individual plates or on a large serving platter and top with the ravioli. Drizzle with more extra-virgin olive oil and sprinkle with fresh oregano leaves and a pinch of salt and freshly ground black pepper. Serve immediately.

# Stuffed Pastas

Despite their many colorful names, all stuffed pastas are essentially made from the same dough, with the shape, size, and the amount of filling varying with the season and region of Italy. Every city and town has its own characteristic forms and stuffings. Agnolotti is from Piedmont, tortellini from Emilia-Romagna, ravioli from Liguria.

What I think is so fun about stuffed pastas is they make you look and feel like an expert chef. And if you use prepared wonton wrappers, they are incredibly easy to make. You can fill them with whatever combination of flavors you like, whether it is a simple mixture of ricotta and herbs, vegetable purées, or finely chopped and seasoned meat or seafood bound with a bit of tomato sauce or béchamel. You can also play around with different shapes and sizes, making mini ravioli to drop into a broth or extra-big ones to serve with a simple brown butter sauce for an elegant starter.

Whichever shape you choose, though, be careful not to overstuff your pasta, or the filling will expand too much and split the pasta when it cooks. Uncooked, stuffed pastas freeze very well, so make a big batch and freeze the extra on baking sheets until completely firm, then transfer to freezer bags to keep for up to three months.

# Orecchiette with Mixed Greens and Goat Cheese

4 servings

Next time you feel like pasta and a salad for lunch, why not combine the two? I love the way the heat of the pasta warms the greens. I often make this when I'm cooking for one; just adjust all the ingredient quantities accordingly, and start with 6 ounces (about 1 cup) of dried pasta.

| | |
|---|---|
| 1 | pound orecchiette (small, disk-shaped pasta) |
| 8 | ounces Mediterranean-style mixed salad greens |
| ½ | cup chopped sun-dried tomatoes (packed in olive oil) |
| 3 | ounces (about ⅓ cup) crumbled fresh goat cheese |
| ½ | cup freshly grated Parmesan cheese |
| ¾ | teaspoon salt |
| ¾ | teaspoon freshly ground black pepper |

Bring a large pot of salted water to a boil over high heat. Add the pasta and cook until tender but still firm to the bite, stirring occasionally, 8 to 10 minutes. Drain the pasta, reserving 1 cup of the pasta water.

Place the salad greens in a large serving bowl and top with the warm pasta and ½ cup of the reserved pasta water. Toss to combine and wilt the greens. Add the sun-dried tomatoes, cheeses, salt, and pepper. Toss to combine, adding the remaining ½ cup of pasta water if necessary. Serve.

# Capellini Piedmontese

4 to 6 servings

Walnut pesto is very popular in Piedmont, where I first tasted this dish. It's really great on its own, simply tossed with a long-cut pasta, but I think the peppers give it a bit more body and also make the dish more beautiful on the plate.

### Walnut Pesto

| | |
|---|---|
| 2 | cups (lightly packed) fresh flat-leaf parsley |
| ¾ | cup toasted walnuts (see page 168) |
| 1 | tablespoon fresh thyme leaves |
| 3 | garlic cloves |
| ½ | cup extra-virgin olive oil |
| ¾ | teaspoon salt, plus more to taste |
| ½ | teaspoon freshly ground black pepper, plus more to taste |

| | |
|---|---|
| 3 | tablespoons extra-virgin olive oil |
| 2 | red bell peppers, cored, seeded, and thinly sliced |
| 1 | orange bell pepper, cored, seeded, and thinly sliced |
| 1 | yellow bell pepper, cored, seeded, and thinly sliced |
| 2 | leeks, thinly sliced crosswise and well rinsed |
| 2 | garlic cloves, finely chopped |
| 1 | pound capellini or angel hair pasta |
| 8 | ounces fontina cheese, cut into small cubes |
| | Salt and freshly ground black pepper to taste |

For the pesto, combine the parsley, walnuts, thyme, and garlic cloves in the bowl of a food processor; blend until finely chopped. With the machine running, gradually add the ½ cup of oil, processing until well blended. Season the pesto with the salt and pepper.

Heat the 3 tablespoons of oil in a large, heavy skillet over medium-high heat. Add the bell peppers, leeks, and the finely chopped garlic. Sauté until the bell peppers are crisp-tender, about 5 minutes.

Bring a large pot of salted water to a boil. Add the capellini and cook until tender but still firm to the bite, stirring often to prevent the pasta from sticking together, about 4 minutes. Drain, reserving 2 cups of the cooking liquid.

In a large bowl, toss the pasta with the pesto, bell pepper mixture, and cheese, adding enough reserved pasta water to moisten. Season to taste with salt and pepper, and serve.

# Spaghetti alla Pirata

4 to 6 servings

*Alla pirata* usually refers to a dish containing seafood, and because pirates were known to be hot-tempered men, the dish is usually spicy as well. You could substitute other seafood you like, such as mussels, squid, or scallops, for either the shrimp or the clams.

| | |
|---|---|
| 1 | (12-ounce) bag cherry tomatoes, halved |
| 3 | scallions (white and pale green parts only), coarsely chopped |
| 3 | garlic cloves |
| | 1-ounce chunk of Parmesan cheese, coarsely chopped |
| 8 | fresh basil leaves, plus ¼ cup chopped fresh basil |
| 3 | tablespoons olive oil |
| | Salt and freshly ground black pepper |
| 1 | pound spaghetti |
| ⅓ | cup extra-virgin olive oil |
| 1 | teaspoon crushed red pepper flakes |
| 1 | pound large shrimp, peeled and deveined |
| 2 | pounds small clams, scrubbed |
| 3 | tablespoons freshly squeezed lemon juice |
| 1 | tablespoon grated lemon zest |

Combine the cherry tomatoes, scallions, garlic, Parmesan, whole basil leaves, and olive oil in the bowl of a food processor. Pulse just until the tomatoes are coarsely chopped (do not purée). Transfer the sauce to a large bowl. Season the sauce with salt and pepper to taste. Set aside.

Bring a large pot of salted water to a boil. Add the spaghetti and cook until tender but still firm to the bite, stirring often to prevent the pasta from sticking together, about 8 minutes.

Meanwhile, whisk the extra-virgin olive oil, red pepper flakes, and ½ teaspoon of salt in a large bowl. Add the shrimp and toss to coat. Heat a large, heavy skillet over high heat. Using a slotted spoon, transfer the shrimp to the hot skillet and sauté just until cooked through and golden, about 2 minutes per side. Transfer the shrimp to a bowl. Add the remaining oil mixture, the clams, and the lemon juice to the same skillet. Cover and cook until the clams open, shaking the pan occasionally, about 8 minutes (discard any that do not open). If the sauce is too liquid, remove the clams and cook over high heat until the sauce is reduced by half.

Drain the pasta and transfer to a large bowl. Add the tomato sauce, and toss to coat. Season the pasta to taste with salt and pepper. Top with the shrimp-and-clam mixture. Sprinkle with the chopped basil and the lemon zest, and serve.

*A note on serving cheese with seafood pastas:* my grandfather would say you should never put cheese on seafood, but I sometimes add a bit of Parmesan to baked seafood pastas, or on a red sauce with seafood, to accent the briny flavors. It's not traditional, but it's delicious. The bottom line? Make your own rules!

# Spaghetti with Red and Yellow Peppers

4 to 6 servings

This is a mildly flavored dish; the peppers virtually melt into the sauce during the long, slow cooking. In my family this is served as a side dish for pork or lamb.

|     |                                                          |
|-----|----------------------------------------------------------|
| 3   | large red bell peppers                                   |
| 3   | large yellow bell peppers                                |
| ¼   | cup extra-virgin olive oil                               |
| 4   | large shallots, thinly sliced (about ¾ to 1 cup)         |
| ½   | teaspoon salt                                            |
| ¼   | teaspoon freshly ground black pepper                     |
| 1   | cup dry white wine                                       |
| 2   | cups reduced-sodium chicken broth                        |
| 1   | pound spaghetti                                          |
| ½   | cup chopped fresh flat-leaf parsley                      |
| ½   | cup grated Parmesan cheese                               |

Preheat the broiler. Cover a heavy baking sheet with foil. Arrange the bell peppers on the baking sheet and broil until the skins brown and blister, turning the peppers occasionally, about 20 minutes. Enclose the peppers in a resealable plastic bag and set aside until cooled to room temperature. Peel and seed the cooled peppers and cut them into strips.

Heat the olive oil in a large, heavy saucepan over medium-low heat. Add the shallots and cook until translucent, about 3 minutes. Add the pepper strips, salt, and pepper and sauté for 5 minutes. Add the wine and chicken broth and continue cooking over low heat for 20 minutes, or until the peppers are very soft.

Meanwhile, bring a large pot of salted water to a boil over high heat. Add the pasta and cook until tender but still firm to the bite, stirring occasionally, 8 to 10 minutes. Drain.

Add the pasta, parsley, and Parmesan cheese to the pepper sauce; stir to combine and coat the pasta. Serve.

# Swordfish and Spaghetti with Citrus Pesto

4 servings

You'll find many recipes for swordfish in Sicily, where it is plentiful, often combined with citrus to give the meaty fish a bit of pizzazz. Here the citrus flavors come from the pesto; it's great over grilled chicken or a steak, too.

| | |
|---|---|
| 1 | pound spaghetti |

**Citrus Pesto**

| | |
|---|---|
| 1 | bunch of fresh basil, stemmed (about 3 cups) |
| ½ | cup toasted pine nuts (see page 168) |
| 1 | garlic clove |
| | Grated zest and juice of 1 lemon |
| | Grated zest and juice of 1 orange |
| ½ | teaspoon salt |
| ½ | teaspoon freshly ground black pepper |
| ½ | cup extra-virgin olive oil |
| 1 | cup freshly grated Parmesan cheese |

**Swordfish**

| | |
|---|---|
| 4 | 6-ounce swordfish steaks |
| | Extra-virgin olive oil |
| | Salt and freshly ground black pepper |

Bring a large pot of salted water to a boil over high heat. Add the pasta and cook until tender but still firm to the bite, stirring occasionally, 8 to 10 minutes. Drain the pasta, reserving ½ cup of the cooking liquid.

Make the pesto: Blend the basil, pine nuts, garlic, lemon zest and juice, orange zest and juice, salt, and pepper in a food processor until finely chopped. With the machine running, gradually add the olive oil until the mixture is smooth and creamy. Transfer to a bowl and stir in the Parmesan. Toss with the warm spaghetti and the reserved pasta water.

Meanwhile, place a grill pan over medium-high heat or preheat a gas or charcoal grill. Brush both sides of the swordfish steaks with olive oil and season with salt and pepper. Grill the swordfish for 3 to 4 minutes on each side for a 1-inch-thick steak.

Transfer the pasta to a serving platter, top with the grilled swordfish, and serve.

# Conghilie with Clams, Mussels, and Broccoli
4 to 6 servings

You don't often see recipes for seafood pastas that incorporate vegetables other than the occasional chopped tomato, but broccoli adds a lot of body, color, and substance to this pasta dish. I love broccoli, but if you don't, feel free to substitute your favorite green vegetable. It's a great quick, elegant meal.

| | |
|---|---|
| 1 | pound conghilie (small shells) pasta |
| 1 | pound broccoli, cut into 1-inch florets (about 4 cups) |
| ¼ | cup olive oil |
| 3 | garlic cloves, minced |
| ⅛ | teaspoon crushed red pepper flakes |
| ½ | teaspoon salt |
| ¼ | teaspoon freshly ground black pepper |
| 1 | pound small littleneck clams, scrubbed |
| 1 | pound mussels, debearded |
| 1 | cup white wine |
| ⅓ | cup chopped fresh flat-leaf parsley |

Bring a large pot of salted water to a boil over high heat. Add the pasta and cook for 6 minutes, stirring occasionally. Add the broccoli to the pasta water and continue cooking until the pasta is tender but still firm to the bite, and the broccoli is blanched, about 4 minutes more. Drain the pasta and broccoli, reserving 1 cup of the cooking liquid.

Meanwhile, heat the olive oil in a large, heavy skillet over medium heat. Add the garlic, red pepper flakes, salt, and pepper, and sauté for 1 to 2 minutes, or until fragrant. Add the clams, mussels, and wine. Cover and cook for 5 minutes, making sure all the shells have opened. (Discard any shells that remain closed.) Sprinkle with the parsley.

In a large bowl, toss together the pasta, broccoli, and shellfish. Add the reserved pasta water, ¼ cup at a time, to moisten, and toss to combine. Transfer to a platter and serve immediately.

# Rotini with Salmon and Roasted Garlic

4 to 6 servings

This may seem like a lot of garlic, but because it's roasted it only contributes a mellow, nutty flavor that goes beautifully with the salmon. Capers and lemon zest add some brightness to the dish, which is a perfect light spring meal.

| | |
|---|---|
| 2 | whole heads of garlic |
| 2 | tablespoons olive oil |
| | Salt and freshly ground black pepper |
| 1 | pound rotini or fusilli (corkscrew-shaped pasta) |
| ½ | cup Marsala or white wine |
| 1 | cup chicken broth |
| 1 | pound salmon, cut into 1-inch cubes |
| | Zest and juice of 1 lemon |
| 1 | tablespoon minced fresh rosemary |
| 2 | tablespoons extra-virgin olive oil |
| 2 | tablespoons drained capers |

Preheat the oven to 400°F.

Cut the heads of garlic in half crosswise and place on a sheet of foil. Drizzle with the olive oil and season with salt and pepper. Fold the foil up and around the garlic, making sure it stays flat, and fold the edges to seal into a tight packet. Roast until soft, about 60 minutes. Let the garlic cool slightly, then squeeze the cloves out of the skin. Mash half of the roasted garlic cloves into a paste with the back of a fork. Set aside.

Bring a large pot of salted water to a boil over high heat. Add the pasta and cook until tender but still firm to the bite, stirring occasionally, 8 to 10 minutes. Drain.

Meanwhile, combine the Marsala and chicken broth in a large, heavy skillet and bring to a simmer. Add the mashed roasted garlic and stir to dissolve. Simmer uncovered for 4 minutes, then add the salmon, cover, and simmer for 4 minutes longer. Remove from the heat and add the remaining whole roasted garlic cloves, the lemon zest and juice, rosemary, and the cooked pasta. Stir to combine; add the extra-virgin olive oil, capers, ½ teaspoon salt, and ½ teaspoon pepper and stir once more. Serve immediately.

# Rigatoni with Red Pepper, Almonds, and Bread Crumbs

4 to 6 servings

The secret ingredient in this dish is the garlicky croutons. I buy good-quality prepackaged garlic croutons from a local bakery and keep them in my pantry for emergencies (I also have been known to snack on them from time to time). You can certainly make them from scratch, but in this dish, it's fine to substitute store-bought if you have a good source. I love the almondy and garlicky flavor the crumbs give the pasta.

| | |
|---|---|
| 1 | pound rigatoni (large, ridged tubular pasta) |
| 3 | cups purchased garlic-flavored croutons (about 5 ounces) |
| ¼ | cup slivered almonds, toasted (page 168) |
| 1 | cup julienned roasted red bell peppers |
| ¾ | cup extra-virgin olive oil |

Bring a large pot of salted water to a boil over high heat. Add the pasta and cook until tender but still firm to the bite, stirring occasionally, 8 to 10 minutes. Drain the pasta and transfer to a large bowl.

Place the croutons and the almonds in a food processor. Pulse until they are finely chopped, with the texture of bread crumbs. Add the crouton-and-almond mixture to the hot pasta along with the peppers and the olive oil. Toss to combine. Serve.

# Angel Hair Pasta with Sun-Dried Tomatoes and Goat Cheese

4 to 6 servings

I love the intensely sweet, chewy flavor of sun-dried tomatoes, and mixed with tomato paste they create a sauce with a very concentrated flavor that doesn't require the long cooking of a traditional tomato sauce. Softened with a bit of goat cheese, this is a creamy sauce that just barely coats the pasta without weighing it down.

| | |
|---|---|
| 1 | (10-ounce) jar sun-dried tomatoes packed in oil, chopped (oil reserved) |
| 1 | small onion, chopped |
| 4 | garlic cloves, minced |
| ¼ | cup tomato paste |
| 1 | cup dry white wine |
| 1 | pound angel hair pasta |
| 3 | tablespoons chopped fresh flat-leaf parsley |
| 1 | teaspoon salt |
| ½ | teaspoon freshly ground black pepper |
| 3-4 | ounces soft fresh goat cheese, coarsely crumbled |

Heat 3 tablespoons of the oil from the sun-dried tomatoes in a large, heavy skillet over medium heat. Add the onion and sauté until tender, about 3 minutes. Stir in the garlic and sauté until fragrant, about 1 minute. Add the tomato paste and cook for 2 minutes, stirring constantly. Add the wine and chopped sun-dried tomatoes and simmer until the liquid reduces by half, about 2 minutes.

Meanwhile, bring a large pot of salted water to a boil. Add the pasta and cook until al dente, stirring occasionally, about 4 minutes. Drain, reserving 1 cup of the cooking liquid. Add the pasta and parsley to the tomato mixture and toss to coat, adding some of the reserved pasta water to moisten. Season the pasta with salt and pepper. Mound the pasta in bowls, sprinkle with the goat cheese, and serve.

# 6

# quick and easy weeknight pastas

If you're like me (and most people) this is the chapter you will rely on the most. No matter how busy we become, we all want to serve meals every night that are fast and easy but still nutritious and pleasing to the eyes and palate. From Little Stars with Butter and Parmesan, a meal so simple the kids can make it for *you,* to Farfalle with Broccoli, which is full of flavor and packs a healthy dose of greens, these are all family-tested favorites that will become part of your weekly repertoire in short order. The key to weeknight pastas is a well-stocked pantry (see page 14 for my recommendations on what you should keep on hand). If you've got a variety of pasta shapes and sizes on hand, plus some canned tomatoes, olive oil, nuts, anchovies, fresh cheese, and herbs, you're never very far away from a well-balanced and completely satisfying meal. If you have a little more time on the weekend, you can make a big pot of marinara or an extra batch of turkey meatballs or pesto to freeze and make weeknight cooking even easier; otherwise, go ahead and use a good-quality jarred marinara or prepared pesto and take pride in the fact that what you are putting on the table is fresh, healthful, and (mostly) homemade.

# quick and easy
# weeknight pastas

Chicken in Lemon Cream with Penne

Little Stars with Butter and Parmesan

Breakfast Scramble with Orzo, Pancetta, and Asparagus

Creamy Orzo

Farfalle with Broccoli

Wagon Wheels with Artichoke Pesto

Spinach Fettuccine with a Quick Sugo or Salsa

Spicy Angel Hair Pasta

Rotelli with Walnut Sauce

Cheesy Baked Tortellini

Cinnamon Pancetta Carbonara

Rigatoni with Sausage, Artichokes, and Asparagus

Linguine with Turkey Meatballs and Quick Sauce

Ditalini with Mushrooms and Artichokes

Mini Penne with Parmesan Chicken

Farfalle with Spicy Sausage and Kale

Penne with Beef and Arugula

Capellini with Tomato and Peas

# Chicken in Lemon Cream with Penne

4 to 6 servings

Both the presentation and flavor of this subtle dish are quite elegant, so while it's easy enough to make for a weeknight dinner, you can certainly serve it to company.

| | |
|---|---|
| 1 | pound penne pasta |
| 3 | tablespoons extra-virgin olive oil |
| 2 | boneless, skinless chicken breast halves, diced into 1-inch cubes |
| 1 | teaspoon herbes de Provence |
| | Pinch of salt, plus ½ teaspoon |
| | Pinch of freshly ground black pepper, plus ¼ teaspoon |
| 1 | cup reduced-sodium chicken broth |
| 2 | cups heavy cream |
| | Zest of 1 lemon |
| | Pinch of cayenne pepper |
| ¼ | cup chopped fresh flat-leaf parsley |
| 1 | tablespoon freshly squeezed lemon juice |

Bring a large pot of salted water to a boil over high heat. Add the pasta and cook until tender but still firm to the bite, stirring occasionally, 8 to 10 minutes. Drain.

Meanwhile, heat the oil in a large, heavy skillet over medium-high heat. Season the cubed chicken breast with the herbes de Provence and a pinch of salt and pepper. Cook the chicken until golden brown, about 5 minutes. Using a slotted spoon, remove the chicken and set aside. Pour off any excess oil from the pan. Add the chicken broth to the pan and cook over medium-high heat, using a wooden spoon to scrape the brown bits off the bottom of the pan. Add the cream, lemon zest, and cayenne. Reduce the heat to medium-low and simmer for 10 minutes.

Add the pasta, chicken, ½ teaspoon salt, ¼ teaspoon pepper, chopped parsley, and lemon juice. Toss to coat the pasta and chicken with the sauce and serve.

# Little Stars with Butter and Parmesan

4 (½-cup) servings

When I was very young, this was my staple dinner; it's an Italian child's comfort food, our version of mac and cheese. It's really easy to make and the ingredients are very simple, which is part of its charm. Serve it to the child in your life, or as a side dish with any kind of roast meat or poultry.

| | |
|---|---|
| 1 | cup (6 ounces) stelline (star-shaped pasta) or other small pasta shapes such as alphabets or riso |
| 4 | tablespoons freshly grated Parmesan cheese |
| 2 | tablespoons unsalted butter, at room temperature |
| | Salt |

Bring a large saucepan of salted water to a boil. Add the pasta and cook until tender but still firm to the bite, stirring often to prevent the pasta from sticking together, about 8 minutes. Drain.

In a large bowl, toss the freshly cooked hot pasta with 2 tablespoons of the cheese until the cheese coats the pasta completely. Add the butter and the remaining 2 tablespoons of cheese. Toss again to coat. Season to taste with salt. Spoon the pasta into small serving bowls and serve immediately.

# Breakfast Scramble with Orzo, Pancetta, and Asparagus

4 servings

The whole idea behind this dish is that it is made from leftovers you find in the refrigerator. This happens to be one of my favorite combinations, but use whatever kind of cheese you find in the bin, and substitute any veggies you have on hand for the asparagus. It's so good that I often make it for a quick dinner when I haven't had a chance to get to the market.

| | |
|---|---|
| ½ | cup orzo (rice-shaped pasta) |
| 10 | large eggs |
| ½ | teaspoon salt |
| ¼ | teaspoon freshly ground black pepper |
| 2 | ounces smoked mozzarella, cut into ½-inch cubes |
| 2 | tablespoons thinly sliced fresh basil |
| 1 | tablespoon unsalted butter |
| 4 | ounces pancetta or bacon, coarsely chopped |
| ½ | cup chopped onion |
| 8 | thin asparagus stalks, trimmed, cut crosswise into ½-inch pieces |

Bring a large saucepan of salted water to a boil. Add the orzo and cook until al dente, stirring occasionally, about 5 minutes. Drain the orzo.

Whisk the eggs, salt, and pepper in a medium bowl to blend. Stir in the cheese and basil. Set aside.

Melt the butter in a large nonstick skillet over medium heat. Add the pancetta and sauté until crisp and golden, about 5 minutes. Add the onion and sauté until tender, about 2 minutes. Add the asparagus and sauté until crisp-tender, about 2 minutes. Add the orzo and stir to coat. Add the egg mixture. Using a rubber spatula, stir the mixture until the eggs are softly set, about 4 minutes.

Transfer the egg mixture to a serving bowl and serve.

# Creamy Orzo

6 to 8 servings

Kids go crazy for this dish. It's creamy, colorful, and, best of all, they can eat it with a spoon!

| | |
|---|---|
| 1 | pound orzo (rice-shaped pasta) |
| 2 | tablespoons olive oil |
| 1 | large shallot, finely chopped |
| 1 | garlic clove, minced |
| 1 | (14.5-ounce) can diced tomatoes, drained |
| 1¼ | cups heavy cream |
| 1 | cup frozen peas, thawed |
| ¾ | cup freshly grated Parmesan cheese |
| | Salt and freshly ground black pepper |

Bring a large, heavy saucepan of salted water to a boil over high heat. Add the orzo and cook until tender but still firm to the bite, stirring often, about 8 minutes. Drain, reserving 1 cup of the pasta water.

Meanwhile, heat the oil in a large, heavy frying pan over medium heat. Add the shallot and garlic, and sauté until tender, about 2 minutes. Add the tomatoes and cook until they are tender, about 8 minutes. Stir in the cream and peas. Add the orzo and toss to coat. Remove the skillet from the heat. Add the Parmesan cheese to the pasta mixture and toss to coat. Stir the pasta mixture until the sauce coats the pasta thickly, adding enough of the reserved pasta water to create a creamy consistency. Season with salt and pepper and serve.

# Farfalle with Broccoli
4 to 6 servings

Anchovy is the secret ingredient that makes this dish so delicious. If you have anchovy haters in your family, don't worry; the anchovies melt into the butter-and-olive oil mixture, so no one will even know they are there.

| | |
|---|---|
| 1 | pound farfalle (bow-tie pasta) |
| 2 | heads of broccoli, trimmed to florets (about 4 cups) |
| ¼ | cup extra-virgin olive oil |
| 4 | tablespoons unsalted butter |
| 3 | garlic cloves, chopped |
| 5 | anchovy fillets, chopped |
| ¼ | teaspoon crushed red pepper flakes |
| ½ | teaspoon salt |
| ½ | teaspoon freshly ground black pepper |
| ½ | cup freshly grated Parmesan cheese |

Bring a large pot of salted water to a boil over high heat. Add the pasta and cook, stirring occasionally. After 5 minutes add the broccoli florets to the pasta, stir, and cook for another 4 minutes. Drain the pasta and broccoli, reserving 1 cup of the pasta water.

Meanwhile, in a large skillet, heat the olive oil and butter over medium-low heat. Add the garlic, anchovies, and red pepper flakes and cook for 5 minutes. Add the broccoli, pasta, salt, and pepper and toss. Add some of the reserved pasta water, if necessary, to make a light sauce. Transfer to a serving platter and sprinkle with the Parmesan cheese.

**Pasta Tip**
For convenience when entertaining, pasta can be prepared earlier in the day and then reheated when it's dinnertime. Cook the pasta until it is al dente, and then scoop it out of the pot of water into a colander. Don't throw out the water. When ready to serve, reheat the water until it is boiling, then add the pasta to the water for a minute. Stir gently with a wooden spoon to loosen the noodles; drain the pasta and toss with sauce.

# Wagon Wheels with Artichoke Pesto

## 4 to 6 servings

Who says pesto has to contain basil—or pine nuts, for that matter? This pesto is luxurious and a pretty, pale green; it makes an unbelievably sophisticated meal in just a matter of minutes. I would also serve this as an elegant first course for a spring meal of lamb or salmon.

| | |
|---|---|
| 1 | pound rotelle (wagon wheel pasta) |
| 1 | (8-ounce) package of frozen artichoke hearts, thawed |
| 1 | cup fresh flat-leaf parsley leaves, lightly packed |
| ½ | cup chopped toasted walnuts (see page 168) |
| | Zest and juice of 1 lemon |
| 1 | garlic clove |
| ½ | teaspoon kosher salt |
| ½ | teaspoon freshly ground black pepper |
| ¾ | cup extra-virgin olive oil |
| ⅔ | cup freshly grated Parmesan cheese |

Bring a large pot of salted water to a boil over high heat. Add the pasta and cook until tender but still firm to the bite, stirring occasionally, 8 to 10 minutes. Drain the pasta, reserving ½ cup of the pasta cooking water.

Meanwhile, in a food processor combine the artichokes, parsley, walnuts, lemon zest and juice, garlic, salt, and pepper. Chop the ingredients fine, stopping the machine a few times to scrape down the sides. With the motor running, drizzle in the olive oil. Transfer the artichoke pesto to a large serving bowl and stir in the cheese. Add the warm pasta and toss to combine. If needed, add the reserved pasta water ¼ cup at a time to moisten the pasta and create a saucelike consistency. Serve.

# Flavored Pastas

You may have noticed a rainbow of pastas on the supermarket shelves recently, as flavored pastas and pastas made from different kinds of flour have become more widely available. Flavored pastas are generally made with the same semolina flour as plain pasta, with the addition of pureed herbs, vegetables, or other ingredients. You'll find green pasta made with spinach or basil, red pasta made with tomatoes or beets, golden pasta flavored with carrot or saffron— even black squid-ink pasta. I love flavored pastas not only because the added ingredients bring another dimension of flavor to a dish, but also because the colors can make a pasta dish so much more fun and festive-looking. Some pastas even combine two or more flavored doughs for a striped effect. This looks especially beautiful when used for stuffed pasta, but you may also find multicolored farfalle or other shapes. Just be sure to check the ingredients to make sure that the pasta is tinted with natural ingredients, not food coloring.

Whole-wheat pasta is another great option if you're looking for a new and different taste in your pasta dishes. This variety of pasta is made from whole-grain flour, meaning the bran and germ of the grain have not been extracted as in refined flours like semolina. The whole grain is nutrient-rich, so it goes without saying that there's a health benefit, but whole-wheat pasta—as well as a constellation of pastas made from alternate grains such as spelt or buck-wheat—also makes for a heartier, earthier dish with a very appealing nutty flavor. Give them a try next time you want to add a new twist to a favorite old pasta recipe.

# Spinach Fettuccine with a Quick Sugo or Salsa

6 to 8 servings

*Sugo* is the Italian word for any kind of sauce. This particular sugo isn't cooked long enough for the tomato chunks to break down completely. Cut the tomatoes into any size pieces you prefer, just as you would for a salsa. If you like it chunky, keep the pieces on the larger side so they won't break up too much when you stir the sauce. Because it is such a basic, straight-forward sauce, it will be a good match to all kinds of flavored pastas, like whole wheat or spinach.

| | |
|---|---|
| 1 | pound spinach fettuccine |
| ¼ | cup extra-virgin olive oil |
| 1 | (28-ounce) can whole San Marzano tomatoes, drained and cut into pieces with kitchen scissors |
| 2 | garlic cloves, whole |
| ¼ | cup chopped fresh flat-leaf parsley |
| ½ | teaspoon salt |
| ½ | teaspoon freshly ground black pepper |
| ⅓ | cup finely chopped fresh basil leaves |

Bring a large pot of salted water to a boil over high heat. Add the pasta and cook until tender but still firm to the bite, stirring occasionally, 8 to 10 minutes. Drain, reserving 1 cup of the pasta water.

In a medium saucepan, warm the olive oil over medium heat. Add the tomatoes, garlic, parsley, salt, and pepper. Cook for 10 minutes. Discard the whole garlic. Add the cooked pasta and toss to coat. Add the reserved pasta water, about ¼ cup at a time, if the pasta needs moistening. Arrange on a serving platter and top with the basil.

# Spicy Angel Hair Pasta

4 to 6 servings

Flavored oils are a pantry staple for me. They add instant flavor, whether I'm making a dressing, a marinade, or a topping for pasta. Chili oil is my favorite because it adds a kick that wakes up your taste buds.

| | |
|---|---|
| 1 | pound angel hair pasta |
| ½ | cup Chili Oil (page 226) |
| ½ | cup chopped fresh flat-leaf parsley |
| 2 | tablespoons grated lemon zest |
| ¼ | cup freshly squeezed lemon juice |
| ½ | teaspoon salt, plus more to taste |
| | Crushed red pepper flakes |
| ⅔ | cup freshly grated Parmesan cheese |

Bring a large pot of salted water to a boil. Add the pasta and cook until tender but still firm to the bite, stirring occasionally, about 8 minutes. Drain, reserving 1 cup of the pasta cooking liquid.

Stir together the chili oil, parsley, lemon zest and juice, and salt in a large bowl. Add the angel hair pasta and toss with enough reserved cooking liquid to moisten; you probably won't need more than ¼ cup or so. Season the pasta with more salt and with red pepper flakes to taste. Transfer to individual bowls, sprinkle with the Parmesan cheese, and serve.

# Rotelli with Walnut Sauce

4 to 6 servings

Rotelli and fusilli are different names for the same, corkscrew-shaped pasta twists. This sauce is essentially a walnut compound butter, and it's a very easy option for those nights when you're not in the mood to do a lot of cooking.

| | |
|---|---|
| 1 | pound rotelli or fusilli (corkscrew pasta) |
| 1½ | cups toasted walnuts (see Note) |
| 2 | tablespoons unsalted butter |
| ¾ | teaspoon salt |
| ½ | teaspoon freshly ground black pepper |
| ¾ | cup extra-virgin olive oil |
| ½ | cup freshly grated Parmesan cheese |
| ½ | cup heavy cream |
| ½ | cup chopped fresh flat-leaf parsley |

Bring a large pot of salted water to a boil over high heat. Add the pasta and cook until tender but still firm to the bite, stirring occasionally, 8 to 10 minutes. Drain the pasta, reserving 1 cup of the cooking liquid.

Meanwhile, in a food processor combine the walnuts, butter, salt, and pepper. Pulse to combine. With the machine running, drizzle in the olive oil in a steady stream. Transfer the mixture to a small bowl and stir in the Parmesan, then the cream.

When the pasta is done, place it in a large bowl while still very warm. Stir in the walnut sauce. Add the reserved pasta liquid, ¼ cup at a time, until the sauce completely coats the pasta, using only as much as needed. Sprinkle with the parsley, toss, and serve.

**Note**

To toast nuts, spread them on a baking sheet and place in a 350°F oven for 5 to 10 minutes, or until fragrant and golden brown; stir them once or twice as they toast and watch to see that they don't get too dark. (You can also toast them in a dry skillet over medium-high heat, tossing as they toast.) Transfer to a bowl to cool.

# Cheesy Baked Tortellini

4 to 6 servings

There are not many meals that are easier than this one, which transforms prepared tortellini and marinara sauce into a rich, savory, comfort-food meal. Just add a salad and you're done.

| | |
|---|---|
| | Olive oil |
| 2 | cups marinara sauce (store-bought or homemade; see page 224) |
| 1/3 | cup mascarpone cheese |
| 1/4 | cup chopped fresh flat-leaf parsley |
| 2 | teaspoons chopped fresh thyme |
| 1 | pound purchased cheese tortellini |
| 2 | ounces thinly sliced smoked mozzarella |
| 1/4 | cup freshly grated Parmesan cheese |

Preheat the oven to 350°F. Lightly oil an 8 x 8 x 2-inch baking dish or 4 individual gratin dishes.

Whisk the marinara sauce, mascarpone cheese, parsley, and thyme in a large bowl to blend. Cook the tortellini in a large pot of boiling salted water until just tender, about 2 minutes. Drain. Add the tortellini to the sauce and toss to coat.

Transfer the tortellini mixture to the prepared baking dish or dishes. Top with the smoked mozzarella cheese and Parmesan cheese. Cover the dish or dishes with foil and bake for 20 minutes, then remove the foil and bake uncovered until the sauce bubbles and the cheeses on top melt, about 10 minutes longer.

# Cinnamon Pancetta Carbonara

6 servings

Fettuccine carbonara is a typical weeknight meal for many Italians, and I love it, too. I couldn't resist adding an extra layer of flavor to this classic dish to improve on something that is already great. I know the sweet-salty combination of bacon with cinnamon sounds odd, but the flavors are extraordinary together. Try it; you'll see.

| | |
|---|---|
| 6 | ounces pancetta (about 6 slices), chopped |
| 2 | ounces bacon (2 or 3 slices), chopped |
| ¼ | teaspoon ground cinnamon |
| 2 | cups heavy cream |
| 1½ | cups freshly grated Parmesan cheese |
| 6 | large egg yolks |
| 18 | ounces fresh fettuccine |
| ½ | teaspoon salt |
| ½ | teaspoon freshly ground black pepper |
| 2 | tablespoons chopped fresh chives |

Cook the pancetta and bacon in a large, heavy skillet over medium-high heat until almost crisp, about 5 minutes. Sprinkle with the cinnamon and sauté until the meat is crisp and golden, about 2 minutes longer. Turn the heat to low. In a small bowl, whisk together the cream, cheese, and egg yolks. Add the cream mixture to the pan with the pancetta and cook at a very low simmer, stirring often with a wooden spoon.

Meanwhile, bring a large pot of salted water to a boil over high heat. Add the fettuccine and cook until it is just tender but still firm to the bite, stirring occasionally, 2 to 3 minutes.

Drain the pasta and add it to the cream mixture with the salt and pepper. Continue cooking over very low heat until the sauce coats the pasta thickly, about 3 minutes (do not boil). Transfer the pasta to a large, wide serving bowl. Sprinkle with the chives and serve.

# Rigatoni with Sausage, Artichokes, and Asparagus

6 servings

Anytime you add sausage to a pasta dish, you exponentially increase the number of people who are going to love it; by adding vegetables, you turn it into a complete meal, a win-win situation all around.

| | |
|---|---|
| ¾ | cup drained oil-packed sun-dried tomatoes, sliced, 2 tablespoons of oil reserved |
| 1 | pound hot Italian sausage, casings removed |
| 2 | (8-ounce) packages frozen artichoke hearts |
| 1 | cup asparagus, trimmed and cut in 1-inch pieces |
| 2 | large garlic cloves, chopped |
| 1¾ | cups chicken broth |
| ½ | cup dry white wine |
| 12 | ounces rigatoni or other tubular pasta |
| ½ | cup shredded Parmesan cheese, plus more for serving |
| ⅓ | cup chopped fresh basil |
| ¼ | cup chopped fresh flat-leaf parsley |
| 8 | ounces fresh mozzarella, cubed (optional) |
| | Salt and freshly ground black pepper |

Heat the oil reserved from the tomatoes in a large, heavy frying pan over medium-high heat. Add the sausage and cook until browned, breaking up the meat into bite-size pieces with a fork, about 8 minutes. Use a slotted spoon to transfer the sausage to a bowl. Add the artichokes, asparagus, and garlic to the same skillet, and sauté over medium heat until the garlic is tender, about 2 minutes. Add the broth, wine, and sun-dried tomatoes. Boil over medium-high heat until the sauce reduces slightly, stirring occasionally, about 8 minutes.

Meanwhile, bring a large pot of salted water to a boil. Cook the pasta in boiling water until tender but still firm to the bite, stirring often, about 10 minutes. Drain the pasta.

Add the pasta, sausage, ½ cup of the Parmesan cheese, the basil, and parsley to the artichoke mixture. Toss until the sauce is almost absorbed by the pasta. Stir in the mozzarella, if using. Season to taste with salt and pepper. Serve, passing the additional Parmesan cheese alongside.

# Linguine with Turkey Meatballs and Quick Sauce
6 to 8 servings

These meatballs are inspired by a turkey meatloaf that I wrap in pancetta before baking. Everyone loves spaghetti and meatballs, though, so I decided to put the pancetta directly into the meatball mixture and bake rather than fry them. The salty pancetta and the sweet sun-dried tomatoes make these meatballs that people will rave about for a long time.

**Turkey Meatballs**

| | |
|---|---|
| 3 | tablespoons olive oil |
| 2 | ounces pancetta, finely diced |
| 1/2 | yellow onion, finely diced |
| 1 | pound ground turkey, preferably dark meat |
| 1/2 | cup freshly grated Romano cheese |
| 1/4 | cup chopped fresh flat-leaf parsley |
| 1/4 | cup plain bread crumbs |
| 1/4 | cup chopped sun-dried tomatoes |
| 2 | eggs, lightly beaten |
| 3/4 | teaspoon salt |
| 3/4 | teaspoon freshly ground black pepper |

| | |
|---|---|
| 1 | pound linguine |
| 1/4 | cup extra-virgin olive oil |
| 1 | (28-ounce) can whole San Marzano tomatoes, drained and cut into pieces with kitchen scissors |
| 2 | whole garlic cloves, peeled |
| 1/4 | cup chopped fresh flat-leaf parsley |
| 1/2 | teaspoon salt |
| 1/2 | teaspoon freshly ground black pepper |
| 1/3 | cup finely chopped fresh basil |

To make the meatballs, preheat the oven to 450°F.

Heat the olive oil in a medium, heavy skillet over medium heat. Add the pancetta and cook for 2 minutes. Add the onion and continue to cook until the pancetta is crisp and the onion is tender, about 4 minutes more. Remove from the heat and let cool.

*(recipe continues)*

In a large bowl, combine the pancetta-and-onion mixture with the remaining meatball ingredients and stir to combine. Form the turkey mixture into balls about 2 inches in diameter, using about 2 tablespoons for each, and place on a foil-lined and greased baking sheet. Bake for 20 minutes.

Bring a large pot of salted water to a boil over high heat. Add the pasta and cook until tender but still firm to the bite, stirring occasionally, 8 to 10 minutes. Drain, reserving 1 cup of the pasta water.

Meanwhile, in a medium saucepan, warm the ¼ cup of olive oil over medium heat. Add the tomatoes, garlic cloves, parsley, salt, and pepper and cook for 10 minutes. Discard the garlic cloves. Add the cooked meatballs and the cooked pasta and toss to coat. Add the reserved pasta water, about ¼ cup at a time, if the pasta needs moistening. Arrange on a serving platter and top with the basil.

# Ditalini with Mushrooms and Artichokes

4 to 6 servings

The literal translation of *ditalini* is "small fingers," and I'm partial to this small, short shape because I like the ingredients in a pasta dish to be all roughly the same size—including the pasta. You can substitute any other small short-cut pasta you have on the shelf.

| | |
|---|---|
| 3 | tablespoons olive oil |
| 1 | small onion, finely chopped |
| 1 | pound mushrooms, trimmed, cleaned, and finely chopped |
| 1 | teaspoon plus ¾ teaspoon salt |
| 1 | cup dry Marsala wine |
| ½ | pound frozen artichoke hearts, thawed |
| ½ | cup heavy cream |
| 1 | pound ditalini or other small, thimble-shaped pasta, such as penneti |
| ¾ | cup freshly grated Parmesan cheese |
| ½ | cup chopped fresh flat-leaf parsley |
| 1 | teaspoon freshly ground black pepper |

Place the olive oil in a large, heavy skillet over medium-high heat. Add the onion and cook for 1 minute. Add the mushrooms and 1 teaspoon of the salt. Sauté, stirring occasionally, until all the moisture has evaporated and the mushrooms have cooked down, about 10 minutes. Add the Marsala and continue cooking until almost all the wine has evaporated, about 5 minutes. Add the artichoke hearts and cream and cook until the artichokes are heated through, about 5 minutes.

Meanwhile, bring a large pot of salted water to a boil over high heat. Add the pasta and cook until tender but still firm to the bite, stirring occasionally, 8 to 10 minutes. Drain the pasta, then add it to the skillet with the mushroom-and-artichoke sauce. Stir in the Parmesan cheese, parsley, and pepper. Transfer to a serving bowl and serve.

# Mini Penne
# with Parmesan Chicken
4 to 6 servings

Another recipe that kids (and adults!) will wolf down, this is a combination of two dishes everyone loves: chicken cutlets Milanese and warm pasta salad.

| | |
|---|---|
| 3 | tablespoons extra-virgin olive oil, plus 1/2 cup |
| 1 | cup buttermilk |
| 1 1/2 | pounds chicken tenders (about 18) |
| 1 | pound mini penne pasta or macaroni |
| 1 1/4 | cups freshly grated Parmesan cheese |
| 3/4 | cup Italian-style seasoned bread crumbs |
| | Salt and freshly ground black pepper |
| 3 | large garlic cloves, minced |
| 3 | tablespoons balsamic vinegar |
| 1/2 | cup chopped fresh flat-leaf parsley |

Preheat the oven to 500°F. Brush a large, heavy, foil-lined baking sheet with 1 tablespoon of oil. Place the buttermilk in a large bowl. Add the chicken tenders, stir to coat, and let stand for at least 15 minutes and up to 30 minutes.

Bring a large pot of salted water to a boil over high heat. Add the pasta and cook until tender but still firm to the bite, stirring occasionally, 8 to 10 minutes. Drain.

Stir the Parmesan and bread crumbs together in a pie pan. Season the mixture with a pinch of salt and pepper. Remove the chicken tenders from the buttermilk, allowing the excess to drip back into the bowl, and dredge them in the bread-crumb mixture to coat completely, pressing to adhere. Arrange the coated chicken tenders on the prepared baking sheets, spacing evenly. Drizzle with 2 tablespoons of the oil and bake until they are cooked through and golden brown, about 12 minutes. Transfer the chicken tenders to a cutting board and cut into 1-inch pieces.

Meanwhile, mash the garlic with 1 teaspoon salt in a medium bowl. Whisk in the vinegar and then the remaining 1/2 cup of oil. Season with 1/4 teaspoon pepper.

Place the drained pasta in a large serving bowl. Drizzle with the vinaigrette, sprinkle with the parsley, and top with the chicken. Toss to combine, and serve.

# Farfalle with Spicy Sausage and Kale

4 to 6 servings

Kale is what makes this pasta a standout. This leafy green is similar to chard and has an assertive flavor that really stands up to the spicy sausages. This was the only way I would eat kale when I was young.

| | |
|---|---|
| 3 | tablespoons olive oil |
| 1 | pound spicy Italian sausage, casings removed |
| 1 | medium onion, chopped |
| 2 | garlic cloves, minced |
| ¼ | pound cremini mushrooms, sliced |
| 1 | (28-ounce) can peeled tomatoes, with juice |
| ¾ | teaspoon salt |
| ½ | teaspoon freshly ground black pepper |
| ¼ | teaspoon crushed red pepper flakes |
| 1 | bunch of kale, stems removed, rinsed, and chopped (about 4 cups) |
| ⅓ | cup heavy cream |
| 1 | pound farfalle pasta |
| | Grated Pecorino Romano cheese, for garnish |

Bring a large pot of salted water to a boil over high heat.

In a large, heavy soup pot, heat the olive oil over medium heat. Add the sausage and cook until golden brown, using a wooden spoon to break the sausage into bite-size pieces. With a slotted spoon, remove the sausage from the pot and set aside. To the same pot, add the onion and garlic and cook over medium heat for 3 minutes. Add the mushrooms and cook until the onion and mushrooms start to brown, about 5 minutes. Add the canned tomatoes with juice. Use a wooden spoon to stir the brown bits off the bottom of the pot and break up the tomatoes. Add the salt, pepper, red pepper flakes, and the sausage.

Meanwhile, blanch the kale in the boiling water for 5 minutes. Use a skimmer to remove the kale from the boiling water and add it directly to the sausage mixture. Reduce the heat and simmer the sauce, covered, for 10 minutes. Add the cream and stir to combine. Remove the mixture from the heat.

While the sauce is simmering, add the pasta to the boiling water. Cook until tender but still firm to the bite, stirring occasionally, 8 to 10 minutes. Drain the pasta, add to the sauce, and toss to combine. Serve with the Pecorino Romano cheese sprinkled on top.

# Penne with Beef and Arugula

## 6 to 8 servings

You can eat this dish right when you make it or serve it an hour or two later at room temperature; the heat of the pasta will warm up the sweet balsamic vinegar and wilt the arugula. It transports quite well, making it a good choice for picnics or buffet spreads.

| | |
|---|---|
| 2 | New York strip steaks, about 8 ounces each |
| | Salt and freshly ground black pepper |
| 1 | teaspoon herbes de Provence |
| 1 | garlic clove, minced |
| ¾ | cup plus 3 tablespoons extra-virgin olive oil |
| 1 | pound penne pasta |
| ¼ | cup balsamic vinegar |
| 2 | tablespoons Dijon mustard |
| ¼ | cup chopped fresh basil |
| ¼ | cup chopped fresh flat-leaf parsley |
| 2 | cups chopped arugula |

Season the steak with salt and pepper, herbes de Provence, and the minced garlic. In a skillet, heat 3 tablespoons of the olive oil over medium heat. Cook the steaks for about 7 minutes per side. Remove the meat to a cutting board and let it rest while you cook the pasta.

Bring a large pot of salted water to a boil over high heat. Add the pasta and cook until tender but still firm to the bite, stirring occasionally, 8 to 10 minutes. Drain the pasta, reserving ¼ cup of the cooking water.

In a small bowl, whisk together the balsamic vinegar, Dijon mustard, ½ teaspoon salt, ½ teaspoon pepper, the basil, parsley, and ¾ cup olive oil. In a large bowl, toss the pasta with half of the salad dressing and the reserved pasta water. Set aside.

Slice the steaks thin and add to the pasta with the arugula. Add more dressing, and season with salt and pepper as needed.

# Capellini with Tomato and Peas

6 servings

Fifteen minutes is all it takes to get this dish on the table and you'll find everything you need in the pantry or in the freezer—no need to shop! It has a very concentrated tomatoey flavor that I find appealing.

| | |
|---|---|
| 1 | pound capellini or other thin spaghetti |
| 3 | tablespoons extra-virgin olive oil |
| 3 | shallots, chopped |
| 2 | garlic cloves, minced |
| 1 | carrot, peeled and diced |
| 1 | teaspoon salt |
| 1 | teaspoon freshly ground black pepper |
| 5 | tablespoons tomato paste |
| ½ | teaspoon dried oregano |
| 1 | teaspoon dried thyme |
| 1 | teaspoon dried parsley |
| 1½ | cups frozen peas, thawed |
| ¼ | cup freshly grated Parmesan cheese |
| ¼ | cup freshly grated Romano cheese |

Bring a large pot of salted water to a boil over high heat. Add the pasta and cook until tender but still firm to the bite, stirring occasionally, 8 to 10 minutes. Drain the pasta, reserving 2 cups of the pasta water.

Meanwhile, heat the oil in a large nonstick frying pan over medium heat. Add the shallots, garlic, carrot, salt, and pepper. Cook until tender, about 8 minutes. Add the tomato paste and ½ cup of the hot pasta water. Stir to melt the tomato paste and create a sauce. Stir in the oregano, thyme, parsley, and peas. Gently fold in the pasta and the cheeses, adding more reserved pasta water if necessary. Transfer to a platter and serve immediately.

# 7

# pasta for special occasions

Even though this book is called *Everyday Pasta,* don't think that you can't serve pasta on your most important occasions. The recipes in this chapter are so rich and decadent—and so universally crowd-pleasing—that they make the perfect centerpiece for any type of get-together. The Spicy Baked Macaroni is my fallback dish for entertaining during awards season or for game nights, and Shrimp Lasagna Rolls with Creamy Marinara makes a beautiful plate for a dinner party. You don't need a group to make most of these, though; some I've put in this section because they take a little more time than most of us can devote to a weeknight meal and are for those nights when you really want to make an effort. Others use fancy ingredients that will make a simple meal just *feel* a little more special, even if you haven't expended any more time or energy to make it. Whichever you choose, rest assured that if your aim is to please and impress, these recipes will do the trick.

# pasta for special occasions

Spicy Baked Macaroni

Tagliatelle and Duck Ragù

Spaghetti with Eggplant, Butternut Squash, and Shrimp

Crab Salad Napoleons with Fresh Pasta

Shrimp Lasagna Rolls with Creamy Marinara

Pork and Lemon Orzotto

Spaghetti with Pinot Grigio and Seafood

Butternut Squash Tortelloni with Cranberry Walnut Sauce

Pappardelle with Seafood Cream Sauce

Champagne Risotto

Linguine and Lobster Fra Diavolo

Corn Agnolotti with Tarragon Butter

Turkey and Cranberry Ravioli

Sweet Fresh Fettuccine

# Spicy Baked Macaroni

8 to 10 servings

When I have friends over to watch sports or an awards show, this is often on the menu. It's comfort food with lots of colorful vegetables and a spicy kick. Make it the day before and reheat it; the flavor improves the longer it sits, which is what you want in a dish for entertaining.

| | |
|---|---|
| 1 | pound elbow macaroni pasta |
| 3 | tablespoons extra-virgin olive oil |
| $\frac{1}{2}$ | pound assorted mushrooms, quartered |
| 1 | onion, chopped |
| 2 | garlic cloves, chopped |
| 1 | (14.5-ounce) can diced tomatoes, with juice |
| 1 | (10-ounce) package frozen spinach, thawed and squeezed dry |
| $\frac{1}{2}$ | teaspoon crushed red pepper flakes |
| $\frac{1}{2}$ | cup bread crumbs |
| $\frac{1}{4}$ | cup plus $\frac{1}{3}$ cup freshly grated Parmesan cheese |
| $\frac{1}{4}$ | cup plus $\frac{1}{3}$ cup freshly grated Romano cheese |
| 2 | tablespoons butter, softened, plus 2 tablespoons cold butter, cut into small pieces |
| 12 | ounces mozzarella cheese, cubed |
| $\frac{1}{4}$ | teaspoon freshly grated nutmeg |

Preheat the oven to 350°F.

Bring a large pot of salted water to a boil over high heat. Add the macaroni and cook until tender but still firm to the bite, stirring occasionally, 8 to 10 minutes. Drain.

Heat the olive oil in a large skillet over medium heat. Add the mushrooms, onion, and garlic. Cook, stirring, until the mushrooms are tender and the onion is golden, about 7 minutes. Stir in the tomatoes, spinach, and red pepper flakes and cook until heated through, about 5 minutes.

In a small bowl, mix together the bread crumbs, $\frac{1}{4}$ cup of the Parmesan cheese, and $\frac{1}{4}$ cup of the Romano cheese. Spread a 9 x 13 x 2-inch glass baking dish with the softened butter and sprinkle half of the bread-crumb mixture inside the dish to coat.

In a large bowl, combine the vegetable mixture with the cooked macaroni, cubed mozzarella, the remaining Parmesan and Romano cheeses, and the nutmeg. Spoon into the baking dish and top with the remaining bread-crumb mix. Dot the top with the 2 tablespoons of cold butter and bake until the top is golden brown, 30 to 40 minutes.

# Tagliatelle and Duck Ragù
4 to 6 servings

When I have time and want a full-flavored pasta dish that reminds me of Sunday dinners at my grandfather's house, this is the recipe I turn to. It will definitely impress your friends and family.

| | |
|---|---|
| 3 | tablespoons olive oil |
| 4 | duck legs, trimmed of excess fat and skin (about 2 pounds) |
| | Salt and freshly ground black pepper |
| ¼ | cup all-purpose flour, for dredging |
| 1 | (14.5-ounce) can diced tomatoes, with juice |
| 1 | medium onion, chopped |
| 1 | carrot, peeled and chopped |
| ½ | cup chopped fresh flat-leaf parsley |
| 2 | garlic cloves |
| 3 | cups beef broth |
| 1 | cup red wine |
| 1 | teaspoon dried thyme |
| 1 | teaspoon dried oregano |
| 1 | pound tagliatelle pasta |
| ¾ | cup freshly grated Parmesan cheese |

In a large, heavy pot, heat the olive oil over medium-high heat. Season the duck legs with salt and pepper, then dredge in the flour. Sear the duck legs until browned, about 4 minutes on the first side and 2 minutes on the second.

Combine the tomatoes, onion, carrot, parsley, and garlic in a food processor and blend until puréed. Carefully pour the mixture into the pot with the duck legs. Stir in the broth, wine, thyme, and oregano, bring to a boil, reduce the heat to low, and simmer, covered, for 1 hour and 15 minutes. Stir, and simmer uncovered for another 1½ hours.

Remove the duck legs from the pot and allow them to cool a bit. Shred the meat and return it to the sauce; discard the bones and skin. Season the ragù with salt and pepper.

Meanwhile, bring a large pot of salted water to a boil over high heat. Add the pasta and cook until tender but still firm to the bite, stirring occasionally, 8 to 10 minutes. Drain the pasta, reserving 1 cup of the cooking liquid, and add the pasta directly to the pot with the duck ragù. Mix well to coat the pasta with the sauce. Add as much of the pasta cooking liquid as needed to moisten the pasta and ragù mixture. Spoon into individual bowls and top with Parmesan cheese.

# Spaghetti with Eggplant, Butternut Squash, and Shrimp
6 servings

The colors in this pasta—the orange of the squash and shrimp against the black eggplant skins—always remind me of Halloween, which is why I often serve it for that holiday. Actually, it's a perfect dish for any celebratory fall meal.

| | |
|---|---|
| ¼ | cup extra-virgin olive oil |
| 1 | large onion, chopped |
| 3 | garlic cloves, finely chopped |
| 1 | small butternut squash, peeled, seeded, and cut into ½-inch pieces (about 5 cups) |
| 2 | Japanese eggplants, cut into 1-inch cubes |
| 1 | tablespoon chopped fresh thyme |
| 1 | teaspoon dried rosemary, crumbled |
| 1½ | cups fish broth or vegetable broth |
| 1¼ | cups dry white wine |
| 2 | pounds uncooked large shrimp, peeled and deveined |
| | Salt and freshly ground black pepper |
| 1 | pound spaghetti |
| ¼ | cup (½ stick) unsalted butter, cut in pieces |

Heat the oil in a large, heavy pot over medium heat. Add the onion and sauté until tender, about 5 minutes. Add the garlic and sauté for just a minute, then add the squash, eggplant, and herbs and sauté until the eggplant softens, 8 to 10 minutes. Add the broth and wine. Bring to a simmer over medium-high heat, then decrease the heat to medium-low and simmer until the squash is tender and the liquid is reduced by about half, stirring occasionally, about 10 minutes. Add the shrimp and simmer gently until almost cooked through, stirring occasionally, about 3 minutes. Season to taste with salt and pepper.

Meanwhile, bring a large pot of salted water to a boil over high heat. Add the pasta and cook until tender but still firm to the bite, stirring often, about 8 minutes. Drain.

Add the cooked pasta, butter, salt, and pepper to the squash mixture, and toss to combine. Transfer the pasta mixture to a wide shallow bowl and serve.

# Crab Salad Napoleons with Fresh Pasta

6 servings

This is one of the prettiest dishes I have ever made. It's perfect for a ladies' lunch, as it's not too heavy and is extremely elegant looking. Make it ahead of time and serve slightly chilled. You could also substitute chopped cooked shrimp for the crab if you prefer.

| | |
|---|---|
| 12 | ounces fresh pasta sheets, purchased or homemade (page 222) |
| 1 | cup mayonnaise |
| 1 | bunch of fresh chives, chopped (about ½ cup) |
| 1 | tablespoon fresh lemon juice |
| ¼ | teaspoon freshly ground black pepper, plus extra for garnish |
| 1 | pound lump crabmeat (about 3 cups), picked over for shells and cartilage |
| 1 | cup frozen peas (about 6 ounces), thawed |
| | Zest of 1 lemon |

Bring a large pot of salted water to a boil over high heat. Add the pasta sheets and cook until tender but still firm to the bite, stirring occasionally, about 2 minutes. Drain the pasta and cool under cold running water. Cut each sheet into 4-inch squares. (You need 18 squares in all.)

In a small bowl, combine the mayonnaise, half of the chopped chives, the lemon juice, and black pepper.

In another, larger bowl, combine the crab and the peas and toss to combine. Add ⅓ cup of the chive mayonnaise mixture and toss gently to combine.

To assemble the Napoleons, place one square of pasta on a plate. Spread a small spoonful of chive mayonnaise on the pasta sheet. Top with ¼ cup of the crab salad and gently spread the salad out to the edges of the pasta square. Top with another sheet of pasta. Spread another spoonful of chive mayonnaise on the pasta square. Top with another ¼ cup of the crab salad and gently spread the salad out to the edges of the pasta sheet. Top with a final pasta square, and add a small dollop of chive mayonnaise. Sprinkle with a pinch of lemon zest, a pinch of the remaining chives, and a grind of black pepper.

Repeat to make 5 more Napoleons.

# Shrimp Lasagna Rolls with Creamy Marinara

6 servings

On my last trip to Venice I fell in love with a shrimp lasagna I tried. This recipe is my twist on that Venetian dish. If you keep frozen shrimp in the freezer, this is a very good way to use them. Be sure not to overcook the lasagna noodles when you are boiling them, as they will finish cooking when you bake the assembled dish. You will only need twelve noodles in all, but cook a few extras in case some break or tear as you are boiling them.

| | |
|---|---|
| 1 | pound lasagna |
| 3 | tablespoons olive oil |
| 1 | pound large shrimp, peeled and deveined |
| | Salt and freshly ground black pepper |
| 3 | garlic cloves, chopped |
| 2 | (15-ounce) containers whole-milk ricotta cheese |
| 1/2 | cup freshly grated Parmesan cheese |
| 2 | eggs, lightly beaten |
| 1/4 | cup chopped fresh basil |
| 1/4 | teaspoon freshly grated nutmeg |
| 3 | cups marinara sauce (store-bought or homemade; see page 224) |
| 1 1/2 | cups grated mozzarella cheese (about 5 ounces) |

Preheat the oven to 350°F.

Bring a large pot of salted water to a boil over high heat. Add the pasta and partially cook until tender but still firm to the bite, stirring occasionally, 6 to 8 minutes. Drain.

Meanwhile, heat the olive oil in a large, heavy skillet over medium heat. Season the shrimp with salt and pepper. Add the shrimp and the garlic to the pan and sauté until the shrimp are cooked, about 4 minutes, stirring often. Remove from the heat and let cool. Coarsely chop the cooled shrimp and place in a large bowl with 2 cups of the ricotta cheese (one container and about one-third of the other), the Parmesan cheese, eggs, basil, 3/4 teaspoon salt, 1/4 teaspoon pepper, and the nutmeg. Stir to combine.

In another bowl, combine the marinara sauce with the remaining 1 cup of ricotta cheese and stir to combine.

To make the lasagna, cover the bottom of a 9 x 13 x 2-inch baking dish with 1 cup of the marinara mixture. Lay four noodles flat on a dry work surface. Spread about 1/4 cup of the

shrimp mixture evenly over each noodle. Roll up and place seam side down in the baking dish. Repeat twice more to make 12 lasagna rolls. Drizzle the rolls with the remaining marinara mixture and top with grated mozzarella. Bake until the lasagna rolls are heated through and the cheese is beginning to brown, about 25 minutes.

# Pork and Lemon Orzotto

4 to 6 servings, depending on how you plate it

When orzo, rice-shaped pasta, is cooked like risotto, it becomes soft and creamy. It's a wonderful foil for pork, as well as chicken or seafood, and you can change the seasonings to match the protein. A drizzle of herby vinaigrette over the pork and orzo gives an extra zing of flavor.

### Orzotto

| | |
|---|---|
| 3½ | cups reduced-sodium chicken broth |
| 3 | tablespoons unsalted butter |
| ¾ | cup finely chopped onion (about 1 onion) |
| 1 | pound orzo pasta |
| ½ | cup dry white wine |
| ¼ | cup freshly grated Parmesan cheese |
| ½ | teaspoon salt |
| ½ | teaspoon freshly ground black pepper |

### Herb Vinaigrette

| | |
|---|---|
| | Zest and juice of 1 large lemon |
| ½ | cup extra-virgin olive oil |
| 3 | tablespoons chopped fresh basil |
| 2 | tablespoons chopped fresh flat-leaf parsley |
| 1 | tablespoon chopped fresh thyme |
| ¼ | teaspoon salt |
| ¼ | teaspoon freshly ground black pepper |
| | Pinch of cayenne pepper |

### Pork Chops

| | |
|---|---|
| 3 | tablespoons olive oil |
| 4 | boneless pork loin chops, about 2 inches thick |
| | Salt and freshly ground black pepper |
| ½ | cup reduced-sodium chicken broth |

For the orzotto, in a medium saucepan, bring the 3½ cups of broth to a simmer over medium-high heat. Cover the broth and keep hot over low heat.

Melt 2 tablespoons of the butter in a large, heavy saucepan over medium heat. Add the onion and cook until tender but not brown, about 3 minutes. Add the orzo and stir to coat with the butter. Add the wine and simmer until the wine has almost completely evaporated, about 3 minutes. Add ½ cup of the simmering broth and stir until almost completely absorbed, about 2 minutes. Continue cooking the pasta, adding the broth ½ cup at a time, stirring constantly and allowing each addition of broth to absorb before adding the next, until the pasta is tender but still firm to the bite and the mixture is creamy, about 20 minutes total.

Meanwhile, combine all the vinaigrette ingredients in a small jar or tight-sealing plastic container. Shake well and set aside.

For the pork, heat the olive oil in a large, heavy skillet over medium-high heat. Season the pork with salt and pepper. When the oil is hot, carefully place the pork chops in the skillet. Sear the pork until a golden crust begins to form, turning once, about 8 minutes per side. Remove the pork from the pan and cover loosely with foil to rest. Pour off the excess oil from the pan and return it to medium heat. Pour the ½ cup of chicken broth into the skillet and, using a wooden spoon, scrape the brown bits off the bottom of the pan. Turn off the heat.

To finish the orzotto, remove the pan from the heat. Stir in the broth from the pork skillet, the Parmesan cheese, the remaining tablespoon of butter, and the salt and pepper.

Spoon the orzotto onto a serving platter (or onto individual plates). Slice each chop into ½-inch-thick strips and arrange the meat on top of the orzotto. Drizzle with the herb vinaigrette. Serve immediately.

# Spaghetti with Pinot Grigio and Seafood
4 to 6 servings

If you love seafood stew, this is the dish for you. It's bright and colorful from the greens and the tomatoes, with lots of great sauce to dip your bread in.

| | |
|---|---|
| 1 | pound spaghetti |
| ¼ | cup olive oil |
| 3 | shallots, chopped |
| 3 | garlic cloves, minced |
| ¾ | cup chopped oil-packed sun-dried tomatoes |
| 1½ | cups Pinot Grigio (or other dry white wine) |
| 1 | pound large shrimp, peeled and deveined |
| 2 | pounds littleneck clams, scrubbed |
| 1 | teaspoon salt |
| 1 | teaspoon freshly ground black pepper |
| 2 | cups arugula, tough stems removed |

Bring a large pot of salted water to a boil over high heat. Add the pasta and cook until tender but still firm to the bite, stirring occasionally, 8 to 10 minutes. Drain.

Meanwhile, heat the olive oil in a large, heavy skillet over medium heat. Add the shallots and garlic and cook for 3 minutes, until tender but not brown. Add the sun-dried tomatoes and cook for another minute. Add the wine, shrimp, and clams and bring the liquid to a boil. Reduce the heat, cover the pan, and simmer until the shrimp are pink and the clams have opened, about 7 minutes. Discard any clams that have not opened.

Add the spaghetti to the skillet with the seafood mixture. Add the salt and pepper and stir to combine, then gently fold in the arugula. Mound the pasta on a serving platter and serve immediately.

# Butternut Squash Tortelloni with Cranberry Walnut Sauce

4 to 6 servings

This recipe has several steps, but give it a try; I think you'll find that none of the steps is difficult, and you can prepare the recipe in stages if you like. Make the filling one day, fill and cook the tortelloni the next, or make and fill the pasta to freeze, and cook anytime you want!

The autumn flavors of squash, nuts, and cranberries make this the perfect side dish for a big holiday meal, or a vegetarian alternative for the non-meat eaters at the table.

### Squash Tortelloni

| | |
|---|---|
| 1 | butternut squash, approximately 2 pounds, peeled and cubed (about 3 cups) |
| 4 | tablespoons extra-virgin olive oil |
| 1½ | teaspoons herbes de Provence |
| ½ | teaspoon salt, plus more to taste |
| ¼ | teaspoon freshly ground black pepper, plus more to taste |
| 2 | large shallots, chopped (about ½ cup) |
| 2 | garlic cloves, chopped |
| 1 | cup whole-milk ricotta cheese |
| 4 | small amaretti cookies, crushed (about ⅓ cup) |
| ¼ | teaspoon freshly grated nutmeg |
| 36 | small square wonton wrappers |

### Cranberry Walnut Sauce

| | |
|---|---|
| ¾ | cup unsalted butter (1½ sticks) |
| 2 | tablespoons coarsely chopped fresh sage |
| ½ | cup dried cranberries, or chopped dried cherries, or a mixture of both |
| ½ | cup toasted walnuts (see page 168), chopped |
| ¼ | teaspoon salt, plus more to taste |
| ¼ | teaspoon freshly ground black pepper, plus more to taste |
| ⅓ | cup freshly grated Parmesan cheese |

To make the tortelloni, preheat the oven to 375°F. On a foil-lined baking sheet, toss together the butternut squash, 2 tablespoons of the olive oil, the herbes de Provence, salt, and

*(recipe continues)*

pepper. Bake until soft and golden, about 25 minutes. Meanwhile, heat the remaining 2 tablespoons of olive oil in a small sauté pan over medium heat. Cook the shallots and garlic until lightly golden, about 3 minutes.

In a food processor, combine the roasted squash, the shallot mixture, and the ricotta cheese and pulse a few times to blend. Add the crushed amaretti cookies and the nutmeg, and sprinkle with salt and freshly ground black pepper. Pulse until smooth. The tortelloni filling can be made one day ahead.

To make the tortelloni, lay out 6 wonton squares, keeping the remaining squares inside the package or under a very lightly dampened paper towel to prevent them from drying out. Place 1 tablespoon of squash mixture in the middle of the square. Using a small pastry brush, wet the edges of the square. Gently fold the square wrapper into a triangle, making sure the edges are securely closed and there are no air pockets inside. Dampen the corners of the longest side of the triangle and gently bring them together, pressing lightly to secure. Place the formed tortelloni on a baking sheet and cover with plastic wrap. Be careful to dry the work surface before laying out another 6 wonton squares; this will help keep the tortelloni from sticking to the baking sheet. Continue until all the squash mixture is used. There should be approximately 36 tortelloni. The tortelloni can be frozen on the baking sheet, transferred to a tightly sealed plastic bag or container, and stored for up to one month.

Bring a large pot of salted water to a boil. As it heats, make the sauce: Melt the butter in a large, heavy skillet over medium heat. Add the sage and cook until the butter starts to brown, about 3 minutes. Turn off the heat and add the cranberries, walnuts, salt, and pepper and stir to combine. Place the tortelloni in the boiling water and gently stir. When they begin to float, they are done, about 3 minutes for fresh, 5 minutes if they've been frozen. Using a slotted spoon, carefully transfer the tortelloni to a serving platter. Top with the cranberry walnut sauce, sprinkle with Parmesan cheese, and serve.

# Pappardelle with Seafood Cream Sauce

4 to 6 servings

This might be the Italian answer to Seafood Newberg: chunks of crab and clams in a rich cream sauce tossed with wide noodles. If you really like clams, it's worth checking to see if you can buy fresh chopped cooked clams at your fish market; the pieces tend to be a little bigger and meatier, with a more subtle, briny flavor than those in cans. The cream sauce is tinted a pretty pink from the tomatoes.

| | |
|---|---|
| 1 | pound pappardelle (wide ribbon pasta) |
| 2 | tablespoons unsalted butter |
| 2 | large shallots, chopped |
| 1/2 | cup dry white wine |
| 1 1/2 | cups heavy cream |
| 1/4 | teaspoon crushed red pepper flakes |
| 1/4 | teaspoon freshly grated nutmeg |
| 1/2 | teaspoon salt |
| 1/4 | teaspoon freshly ground black pepper |
| 8 | ounces lump crabmeat (about 1 1/2 cups), picked over for bits of shell and cartilage |
| 1 | (6.5-ounce) can chopped clams, drained |
| 2 | large tomatoes, seeded and chopped (about 1 cup) |
| 1/4 | cup chopped fresh chives (about 1/2 bunch) |

Bring a large pot of salted water to a boil over high heat. Add the pasta and cook until tender but still firm to the bite, stirring occasionally, 8 to 10 minutes. Drain the pasta, reserving 1 cup of the pasta cooking water.

Meanwhile, melt the butter in a large, heavy skillet over medium heat. Add the shallots and cook until the shallots soften, about 2 minutes. Add the wine and cook until it is almost evaporated, about 3 minutes. Add the cream, red pepper flakes, nutmeg, salt, and pepper and continue cooking over medium heat for 5 minutes. The sauce should begin to thicken.

Add the crab, clams, and tomatoes and stir to combine. Add the pasta and toss. If necessary, add 1/2 cup of the reserved pasta water at a time to create a more luscious sauce. Transfer to a serving platter or individual plates and sprinkle with the chopped chives.

# Champagne Risotto

2 servings

If you're cooking for someone special, you won't find many dishes more romantic than this one. It looks sophisticated, tastes rich, and makes a real statement. It's one of my standbys when I want to make a cozy dinner for me and my husband.

| | |
|---|---|
| 4 | thin slices prosciutto |
| 3 | cups reduced-sodium chicken broth |
| 12 | asparagus spears, cut diagonally into 1-inch pieces |
| 2 | tablespoons unsalted butter |
| 1 | shallot, finely chopped |
| ¾ | cup Arborio rice or medium-grain white rice |
| ¾ | cup champagne |
| ¼ | cup freshly grated Parmesan cheese |
| ¼ | teaspoon salt |
| ½ | teaspoon freshly ground black pepper |

Preheat the oven to 450°F. Place the prosciutto slices on a lightly greased baking sheet. Bake until the prosciutto slices are almost completely crisp, 6 to 8 minutes. The slices will crisp up even more as they cool. Set aside.

In a medium saucepan, bring the chicken broth to a boil. Reduce the heat and simmer the broth. Blanch the asparagus in the chicken broth for 2 minutes. Remove the asparagus with a slotted spoon. Set the asparagus aside and keep the chicken broth at a low simmer.

In another medium saucepan, melt 1 tablespoon of the butter. Add the shallot and cook until tender, about 3 minutes. Add the Arborio rice and stir to coat in the butter. Continue toasting the rice, stirring constantly, for about 3 minutes more. Add the champagne and simmer until the champagne has almost evaporated, about 3 minutes. Add ½ cup of the simmering broth and stir until almost completely absorbed by the rice, about 2 minutes. Continue cooking the rice, adding the broth ½ cup at a time, stirring constantly and allowing each addition of broth to absorb before adding the next, until the rice is tender but still firm to the bite and the mixture is creamy, about 20 minutes total. Remove from the heat.

Gently stir in the asparagus, the remaining tablespoon of butter, the Parmesan, salt, and pepper. Spoon the risotto into serving dishes and garnish by breaking the crisp prosciutto into smaller pieces over the risotto.

# Reimagining Risotto

Though not a pasta, risotto is similar in how and when it is cooked and served. It is one of those dishes that just about everyone loves, and because it is rather labor intensive, it shows you've gone to some effort. (For that reason, it's not the best choice for a large gathering; save it for an intimate dinner with someone special or a small group.)

The creamy, comforting texture of Arborio and other short-grain rices presents the perfect neutral canvas for showcasing luxurious ingredients like lobster or truffles, and it's also a dish that welcomes improvisation and creativity. The only true given in a risotto recipe is the rice; you can vary the liquid and flavors almost infinitely. Chicken stock is the liquid most typically used in risotto, but beef, fish, or vegetable stocks all work perfectly as well. Beyond stocks, you can make your risotto with red or white wine or fruit juices, such as pomegranate, orange, or lemon, or tomato juice, all depending on what other ingredients you will be adding. The technique is the same no matter what liquid or flavorings you add; just watch the risotto carefully to prevent scorching or sticking if you are using ingredients that contain sugar (including dairy products). Here are a few fun combinations to get your imagination flowing:

**Red Wine Risotto with Peas:** The rice takes on the wine's deep red color.

**Chocolate Risotto:** Cook the rice with milk, stirring in sugar, chopped hazelnuts, chocolate chips, raisins, and brandy for the last five minutes of cooking.

**Cinnamon Peach Risotto:** Replace the stock with heavy cream, and flavor with ground cinnamon, sliced peaches, and brandy.

**Lemon Pomegranate Risotto:** Use pomegranate juice as your liquid, and flavor with lemon zest at the end.

**Risotto with Gorgonzola:** Use a combination of heavy cream and stock, and stir in crumbled Gorgonzola cheese and cranberries before serving.

**Surf and Turf Risotto:** Prepare the rice with seafood or fish stock; just before serving, add sliced smoked sausage, ham, cooked shrimp, and sautéed mushrooms to warm through.

**Strawberry Risotto:** Replace the stock with orange juice, and garnish with sliced strawberries and chopped mint.

# Linguine and Lobster Fra Diavolo

4 servings

This is a decadent dish that is very popular with my family at Christmas-time, when pasta with seafood is a holiday tradition for Italians. For others, though, it's a reminder of summers on the Cape or in the Hamptons. Whatever memories it may conjure for you, we can all probably agree that it is a rich, sophisticated dish that puts a smile on the face of anyone who tastes it.

| | |
|---|---|
| 1 | pound linguine |
| 3 | tablespoons olive oil |
| 1 | medium onion, finely chopped |
| 3 | garlic cloves, finely chopped |
| 1/2 | teaspoon crushed red pepper flakes |
| 1/2 | teaspoon salt |
| 1/2 | teaspoon freshly ground black pepper |
| 1/4 | teaspoon dried oregano |
| 1/2 | cup Cognac |
| 1 | (14.5-ounce) can diced tomatoes, with juice |
| | Tail and claw meat from 2 cooked 1½-pound lobsters, tail meat cubed |
| 3 | tablespoons chopped fresh flat-leaf parsley |
| 3 | tablespoons chopped fresh basil |
| 4 | fresh basil sprigs, for garnish |

Bring a large pot of salted water to a boil over high heat. Add the pasta and cook until tender but still firm to the bite, stirring occasionally, 8 to 10 minutes. Drain the pasta.

Meanwhile, in a large, heavy skillet heat the olive oil over medium-high heat. Add the onion and cook for 4 minutes. Add the garlic, red pepper flakes, salt, pepper, and oregano. Stir and cook for 1 minute. Add the Cognac, using a wooden spoon to scrape up the brown bits from the bottom of the pan. Add the tomatoes, lobster, parsley, and chopped basil. Cook until the lobster meat and tomatoes are heated through, 2 to 3 minutes.

Add the linguine to the pot and stir to coat the pasta in the sauce. Transfer into individual pasta bowls, reserving one claw for each bowl. Place the claw on top of the pasta and place a basil sprig next to it. Serve immediately.

# Corn Agnolotti with Tarragon Butter

4 to 6 servings (about 40 agnolotti)

Creamed corn has never been so sophisticated! This delicate, creamy filling deserves the equally subtle flavor of good, fresh pasta, so make this sometime when you are inspired to make your own pasta, or if you find a source for really fresh, homemade pasta sheets.

### Corn Agnolotti

| | |
|---|---|
| ¼ | cup cornmeal |
| 1 | recipe Fresh Pasta (page 222) |
| 2 | (14.75-ounce) cans creamed corn, drained well |
| ½ | cup mascarpone cheese (4 ounces) |
| ¼ | cup soft fresh goat cheese (2 ounces) |
| ½ | teaspoon chopped fresh tarragon |
| ¼ | teaspoon freshly ground black pepper |
| 1 | egg, for egg wash |

### Tarragon Butter

| | |
|---|---|
| ½ | cup (1 stick) unsalted butter, at room temperature |
| ⅓ | cup corn kernels (fresh or canned) |
| 1 | teaspoon chopped fresh tarragon |
| ½ | teaspoon grated lemon zest |
| ¼ | teaspoon salt |
| ¼ | teaspoon freshly ground black pepper |
| ¼ | cup freshly grated Parmesan cheese |

Sprinkle a baking sheet with some of the cornmeal and set aside. Cut the ball of pasta dough into 8 equal pieces. Shape each piece into a rectangle about the size of a deck of cards. Cover the dough with plastic wrap while you are working. Roll a rectangle of dough through the widest setting of a pasta machine 3 times, until it is smooth. Continue rolling it through, decreasing the setting each time until you have reached the thinnest setting. Sprinkle the sheet lightly with cornmeal, gently fold it, and set it on the cornmeal-lined baking sheet. Cover with plastic wrap. Continue rolling out the rest of the pasta until all 8 pieces have been rolled out.

*(recipe continues)*

In a medium bowl, mix together the drained creamed corn, mascarpone cheese, goat cheese, tarragon, and pepper. Stir to combine and set aside. In a small bowl, beat the egg with 1 tablespoon water.

To form the agnolotti, place a sheet of pasta on a dry work surface. Using a pastry brush, brush the entire sheet of fresh pasta with the egg wash. Place rounded teaspoons (about 1 ounce) of the corn filling on the pasta sheet, about 2 inches apart. Carefully place another sheet of pasta over the mounds, smoothing out any air pockets and firmly sealing the pasta around the filling. Using a scalloped pasta cutter (or a sharp knife), cut the pasta into small squares. Transfer the agnolotti to the cornmeal-lined baking sheet. Continue forming the remaining agnolotti.

To serve, bring a large pot of salted water to a boil over high heat. Add the pasta and cook until they float, about 2 minutes. While the pasta cooks, gently mix together all the tarragon butter ingredients in a medium serving bowl. Drain the pasta, using a large mesh strainer or slotted spoon, and transfer them to the serving bowl with the tarragon butter. Toss to coat. Sprinkle with the Parmesan cheese and serve immediately.

# Turkey and Cranberry Ravioli

6 to 8 servings

When Todd and I are craving the flavors of Thanksgiving—or when we're spending the holiday alone and I'm not in the mood to cook a whole turkey just for the two of us—I make these holiday-worthy ravioli. They look and taste festive, and there are never any leftovers!

### Turkey Ravioli

| | |
|---|---|
| 1 | pound ground turkey, preferably dark meat |
| 1/2 | cup whole-berry cranberry sauce |
| 1/2 | cup freshly grated Romano cheese |
| 1/4 | cup bread crumbs |
| 1/4 | cup chopped fresh flat-leaf parsley |
| 2 | eggs |
| 1 | teaspoon salt |
| 1 | teaspoon freshly ground black pepper |
| 80 | small square wonton wrappers |

### Gravy

| | |
|---|---|
| 3/4 | cup (1 1/2 sticks) unsalted butter |
| 4 | shallots, chopped |
| 1/4 | cup all-purpose flour |
| 3 | cups reduced-sodium chicken broth |
| 1/2 | cup heavy cream |
| 1/2 | cup grated Romano cheese, plus more for serving |
| 1/4 | cup finely chopped fresh flat-leaf parsley |
| 1 | teaspoon salt |
| 1 | teaspoon freshly ground black pepper |

To make the ravioli, stir together the turkey, cranberry sauce, cheese, bread crumbs, parsley, eggs, salt, and pepper in a medium bowl. Place 10 wonton wrappers on a work surface. Brush lightly with water using a pastry brush. Place 1 tablespoon of the turkey mixture on each of the wonton wrappers. Top each with another wonton wrapper. Push out any air bubbles, then press the edges tightly to seal. Repeat with the remaining filling and wrappers, forming 10 ravioli at a time.

To make the gravy, heat the butter in a medium, heavy skillet over medium heat. Add the shallots and cook until tender, about 4 minutes. Add the flour and stir until cooked, about

1 minute. Slowly add the chicken broth, stirring quickly to avoid lumps, and simmer for 3 minutes, stirring often. Stir in the cream, cheese, parsley, salt, and pepper.

Meanwhile, bring a large pot of salted water to a boil over high heat. Add the ravioli and cook until tender but still firm to the bite and the filling is cooked, about 3 minutes, stirring occasionally. Use a skimmer to remove half the ravioli and transfer them to individual plates or a serving platter. Drizzle them with some of the gravy to keep them from sticking together. Drain the remaining ravioli and drizzle with the remaining gravy. Sprinkle with cheese and serve immediately.

# Dried Pasta Versus Fresh

Fresh pastas can now be found in the refrigerated cases of many supermarkets, and you may also be able to purchase fresh pasta and pasta sheets at your local Italian market or gourmet shop. Don't assume that fresh pasta is necessarily preferable to dried, though; for many dishes the smooth, firm surface and chewy texture of dried pasta is the better choice. Reach for the fresh pasta when you are serving a more delicate sauce, such as mild, creamy preparations or one based on butter, which complements its softer texture.

Both types of pasta are made from the same ingredients: flour, salt, and water. However, dried pastas are made with hard wheat flour, called semolina, while fresh pasta generally uses a softer flour that is lower in protein and makes a softer noodle. Some fresh pastas also include egg, which contributes both richness and a warm yellow color.

Because dried semolina pasta doesn't absorb sauce the way more porous fresh pastas do, they work best with tomato- or oil-based sauces and should be cooked together with the sauce briefly to meld their flavors. Fresh pasta should be cooked quickly (monitor it carefully as it can overcook in a matter of seconds) and then tossed with the sauce in a serving bowl; don't cook the two together or the dish will become gummy.

# Sweet Fresh Fettuccine

4 breakfast servings or 6 appetizer or dessert servings

My grandfather would occasionally make this for us as a special breakfast treat when I was young; now I serve it as an unusual first course for a fancy dinner or even, occasionally, for dessert. It's very unexpected—and very delicious. Serve it in small portions, as it is quite rich.

| | |
|---|---|
| 2 | cups heavy cream |
| | Zest of 1 lemon |
| | Zest of 1 orange |
| 2 | tablespoons honey |
| | Pinch of kosher salt |
| ½ | recipe of Fresh Pasta (page 222), cut into fettuccine, or 12 ounces purchased fresh pasta or dried fettuccine (see Note) |
| 1 | tablespoon freshly squeezed lemon juice |
| ¼ | cup chopped toasted hazelnuts (see page 168) |

Bring a large pot of salted water to a boil over high heat.

In a large, heavy skillet, heat the cream, zests, honey, and salt over medium heat, being careful not to let it boil. Cook at a bare simmer, stirring occasionally, for about 4 minutes.

Meanwhile, add the pasta to the boiling water and cook until tender but still firm to the bite, stirring occasionally, 2 to 3 minutes. Drain the pasta well, then add it and the lemon juice to the skillet with the cream sauce. Toss to combine.

Divide the pasta among 4 to 6 shallow bowls and sprinkle with the hazelnuts. Serve immediately.

Note
If using dried pasta, substitute
1 pound dried, cooked in a large pot
of salted boiling water until just
al dente. Add to the cream sauce as
above and cook gently in the sauce for
another 3 minutes, or until the pasta
has absorbed most of the sauce.

pasta

# basics

# 8

# basic recipes

This section provides you with all the fundamentals you need to put a great pasta meal on the table: essential sauces like marinara and béchamel as well as my favorite flavored oils and vinaigrettes I reach for time and again. If you want to try your hand at making your own fresh pasta, this is where you'll find the recipe. You'll also find some great pointers on choosing an Italian wine to complement your meal and a few menu ideas to help you round out everything. Enjoy!

# Fresh Pasta
## makes 1½ pounds

For a richer yet more delicate flavor, nothing beats freshly made pasta. It takes a bit of time—and a pasta-rolling machine—but the results are worth the effort.

It is certainly possible to buy good-quality fresh pasta, either in sheets or cut into noodles. But like making your own bread, making fresh pasta is a very satisfying way to spend a Sunday afternoon. I especially enjoy preparing fresh pasta at the holidays or when I have family over and everyone can get involved.

| | |
|---|---|
| 3 | cups all-purpose flour |
| 4 | large eggs |
| 1 | tablespoon kosher salt |
| 1 | tablespoon olive oil |

Place the flour in the bowl of a food processor. In a small bowl, lightly beat the eggs. Add the salt and olive oil to the eggs and stir to combine. Add the egg mixture to the food processor with the flour and pulse to combine the ingredients, scraping down the sides once or twice. Continue, with the machine running, until the liquid is evenly distributed, about 1 minute. The dough should stick together if pinched between your fingers and be cornmeal yellow in color. Some of the dough will be clumping together, but it will not form a ball.

Turn the dough out onto a lightly floured surface. Gather the dough into a ball and knead gently until the dough is smooth. Cover with plastic wrap and let rest for 30 minutes before rolling and shaping as desired.

# Basic Marinara Sauce
*makes about 2 quarts*

Every cook should have a good marinara sauce in his or her repertoire, and I think this one is just about perfect. Though not as quick to throw together as some of the other tomato sauces I depend on (see page 164 for a really quick, basic *sugo*), the time you invest in making it will be repaid with a full-flavored, robust sauce that can be used in dozens of different ways. The sauce freezes very well, so why not make a double batch to freeze (after cooling completely) in 2-cup portions? Frozen sauce may be stored for up to 3 months.

| | |
|---|---|
| ½ | cup extra-virgin olive oil |
| 2 | small onions, finely chopped |
| 2 | garlic cloves, finely chopped |
| 2 | celery stalks, finely chopped |
| 2 | carrots, peeled and finely chopped |
| ½ | teaspoon sea salt, plus more to taste |
| ½ | teaspoon freshly ground black pepper, plus more to taste |
| 2 | (28-ounce) cans crushed tomatoes |
| 2 | dried bay leaves |

In a large pot, heat the oil over medium-high heat. Add the onions and garlic and sauté until the onions are translucent, about 10 minutes. Add the celery, carrots, and ½ teaspoon each of salt and pepper. Sauté until all the vegetables are soft, about 10 minutes. Add the tomatoes and bay leaves, and simmer uncovered over low heat until the sauce thickens, about 1 hour. Remove and discard the bay leaves. Season the sauce with more salt and pepper to taste. (The sauce can be made 1 day ahead. Cool, then cover and refrigerate. Rewarm over medium heat before using.)

# Béchamel Sauce
makes about 4 cups

This basic white sauce is what gives many pasta dishes, like lasagna, a rich creamy texture. It's not hard to make and you'll find lots of uses for it.

| | |
|---|---|
| 5 | tablespoons unsalted butter |
| 1/2 | cup all-purpose flour |
| 4 | cups warm whole milk |
| 1/2 | teaspoon salt |
| 1/4 | teaspoon freshly ground white pepper |
| | Pinch of freshly grated nutmeg |

In a medium saucepan, melt the butter over medium heat. Add the flour and whisk until smooth, about 2 minutes. Gradually add the warm milk, whisking constantly, until the sauce is thick, smooth, and creamy, about 10 minutes (do not allow the béchamel sauce to boil). Remove from the heat and stir in the salt, pepper, and nutmeg. (The sauce can be made up to 3 days ahead. Cool, then cover and refrigerate.)

# Arrabbiata Sauce
makes about 5 cups

| | |
|---|---|
| 2 | tablespoons extra-virgin olive oil |
| 6 | ounces sliced pancetta, coarsely chopped |
| 2 | teaspoons crushed red pepper flakes |
| 2 | garlic cloves, minced |
| 5 | cups marinara sauce (store-bought or homemade; see page 224) |

Heat the olive oil in a large soup pot over medium heat. Add the pancetta and sauté until golden brown, about 5 minutes. Add the red pepper flakes and garlic and sauté until tender, about 1 minute. Add the marinara sauce and bring to a simmer, then remove from the heat and let cool until ready to use.

# Chili Oil
makes ½ cup

This simple recipe is not only great for bread-dipping, but can also be used to liven up the flavors in other dishes—as your cooking oil, or in salad dressing, or as a pasta topping, or just drizzled over grilled fish or meat.

½   cup olive oil
1   teaspoon crushed red pepper flakes

In a small, heavy saucepan, heat the oil and red pepper flakes over low heat, stirring occasionally, until a thermometer inserted into the oil registers 180°F, about 5 minutes. Remove from the heat and let cool to room temperature, about 2 hours. Transfer the oil and pepper flakes to a 4-ounce bottle or other small container and seal the lid. Refrigerate up to 1 month.

# Citrus Olive Oil
makes about ½ cup

½   cup olive oil
2   tablespoons fresh lemon juice
1   tablespoon fresh orange juice or tangerine juice

Place all of the ingredients in a tight-lidded jar and shake to combine. Refrigerate for up to 1 month.

# Roasted Garlic Vinaigrette

makes ½ cup

This is a robust dressing that is good with strongly flavored greens like escarole or spinach. It's also very good on grilled foods and vegetables like potatoes, or as a dressing for chicken and pasta salad. Because the garlic thickens the dressing and gives it body, less oil is needed than for a conventional vinaigrette.

| | |
|---|---|
| 1 | whole head of garlic |
| 2 | tablespoons olive oil |
| | Salt |
| 2 | tablespoons chopped fresh parsley |
| ¼ | cup balsamic vinegar |
| ¼ | cup extra-virgin olive oil |
| | Pinch of sugar |
| ¼ | teaspoon freshly ground black pepper |

Preheat the oven to 400°F.

Cut the head of garlic in half cross-wise and place it cut side up on a sheet of foil. Drizzle it with olive oil and sprinkle it with salt. Fold the foil up and around the halves of garlic, making sure they stay flat. Seal the foil into an airtight package. Roast until golden and soft, about 60 minutes. Let the garlic cool slightly in the foil.

Squeeze the garlic cloves out of their skins into a blender. Add the parsley and balsamic vinegar and pulse together until blended. Drizzle the extra-virgin olive oil into the blender while the machine is running. Add the sugar, ½ teaspoon salt, and pepper and blend until incorporated.

# Red Wine Vinaigrette
makes 1½ cups

This is the classic salad dressing, one I rely on all the time not only for salads but as a marinade for meats, to drizzle on crostini, and more.

- ½ cup red wine vinegar
- 3 tablespoons freshly squeezed lemon juice
- 2 teaspoons honey
- 1 cup extra-virgin olive oil
- ½ teaspoon salt
- ½ teaspoon freshly ground black pepper

Combine the vinegar, lemon juice, and honey in a blender. With the motor running, gradually add the oil. Season the vinaigrette with salt and pepper, adding more to taste if needed.

# Parmesan Frico
makes 12

I love these cheesy, salty, crispy wafers not only because they are so yummy, but because they are so versatile. I put them in bread baskets, add them to soups, and serve them topped with scoops of salad.

- 1 cup freshly grated Parmesan cheese
- 1 teaspoon freshly ground black pepper

Preheat the oven to 375°F. Line a baking sheet with parchment paper. Place tablespoon-size mounds of Parmesan on the paper at least 2 inches apart. Gently flatten each mound of cheese with the bottom of a glass or the back of a spoon and sprinkle with black pepper. Bake for 10 minutes, or until the cheese has spread out to a 1- to 1½-inch round and is bubbling and golden around the edges. Place the baking sheet on a wire rack to cool the frico completely.

# Italian Wine
## A Crash Course by Christian Navarro

The late, great winemaker Giacomo Conterno once said, "Wine nourishes the soul." To me there is nothing more satisfying than an excellent plate of pasta matched to perfection with a simple glass of wine. Together they spark an explosion of flavors far beyond what each can provide on its own. Of course, nothing pairs better with an Italian meal than an Italian wine, although for many wine buyers a stroll down the Italian aisle of their wine store can be confusing. Once you've learned a bit about them, though, you'll find there is an exciting gamut of Italian wines beyond Chianti and Pinot Grigio.

The history of wine in Italy spans more than twenty-eight centuries, back to the eighth century B.C., when the ancient Greeks settled in southern Italy. (In fact the Greeks were so impressed with the Italian climate they named the region Oenotria, land of the trained vine.) I can think of few places where wine is more seamlessly woven into the fabric of everyday life than in Italy; it is as much a part of life there as is pasta or tomatoes. And while Italy produces some of the world's finest (and most costly) wines, it is hardly a pleasure that is reserved for the elite. In a country where the vintner may also be the pasta maker and the cook, Italian wine is best enjoyed at the lunch and dinner table. Just as wine enhances the food, the food enhances the wine, creating a marriage of flavors for all the senses.

The styles and flavors of Italian wines vary greatly from north in the snowy Alps to south at the sunny shores of the Mediterranean. Much like the food, the wines reflect the landscape of the people, the weather, and the geographic location. Northern regions like Piedmont, Lombardy, and Alto Adige produce wines that tend to be more reserved, refined, and perfumed. Toward the center of Italy in Tuscany and Umbria the wines gain in exuberance and sophistication. Down in the warmest parts of Italy like Apulia, Sicily, and Sardinia, the wines tend to be extremely flavorful, spicy, and almost sunbaked in style.

When selecting wine to complement Italian food, both Giada and I seek out wines we enjoy. There are no rules, just enjoyment. Wine can be complex and intimidating if you let it, so don't. Wine is fun! Whether you are celebrating an important event or just cooking an everyday meal at home, the most important thing is to remember what you like: If you like it, it is good. It's just that easy. That said, there are a few helpful hints to guide you on this journey of enjoyment of Italian wine. The key is keeping it simple, much as they do in Italy. You can never go wrong if you follow what I call the body and flavor rules. Reduced down to its purest terms, that means the lighter the course, the lighter the wine; the more flavorful the course, the more flavorful the wine. This rule applies equally to white, red, sparkling, and dessert wines.

When choosing a wine to serve with your pasta, ask yourself about the overall meal. Is it a light, delicate menu or is it a hearty, robust repast? The goal is to match the two. For example: Giada's Pappardelle with Lamb Stew brings to mind sitting by the wood-burning stove on a cold rainy night in Alba as the rich aroma of a savory ragù fills the air. To match the stew, a hearty-style wine like those made in Barolo and Barbaresco from the Nebbiolo grape would be a fitting partner as they tend to be full-bodied and full-flavored, and have a warming effect. On the lighter side, I might choose a more elegant and delicate wine, like a Pinot Bianco or Pinot Grigio from the

Alto Adige or Friuli areas, to pair with her Rotini with Salmon and Roasted Garlic; either wine would be a perfect foil and enhancement for the richness of the fish and the sweetness of the roasted garlic.

At right is a cheat sheet listing the primary characteristics of some of the most popular Italian wines. It will tell you whether a particular wine is light, medium, or heavy in body, as well as the key flavor note, from spicy to fruity, delicate to zesty. Using these cues, you can easily find a wine that will mirror the tone of your meal to a tee. When in doubt, though, I always recommend consulting a professional. I have been in the business for more than twenty years, but when I am on the road in a small village in the middle of a remote area shopping for wine and food, I occasionally find myself stumped as to the ideal wine to go with my dinner. I never hesitate to ask someone who might be able to give a little advice based on what I am cooking that night. Invariably I discover something new and exciting that tastes great—and pay far less than I expected.

Happy cooking and happy tasting!

# Reds

**Nebbiolo** (medium, zesty)
**Barbaresco** (heavy, zesty)
**Sangiovese** (light, fruity)
**Barolo** (heavy, zesty)
**Barbera** (medium, zesty)
**Dolcetto** (light, fruity)
**Valpolicella** (light, zesty)
**Amarone** (heavy, spicy)
**Chianti** (medium, zesty)
**Nero d'Avola** (medium, spicy)
**Montepulciano** (medium, fruity)
**Brunello di Montalcino** (heavy, zesty)
**Aglianico** (heavy, spicy)
**Super Tuscan** (heavy, zesty)
**Syrah** (heavy, spicy)

# Whites

**Pinot Grigio** (light, delicate)
**Chardonnay** (heavy, zesty)
**Pinot Bianco** (medium, zesty)
**Sauvignon** (light, fruity)
**Tocai Fruliano** (light, delicate)
**Arneis** (medium, zesty)
**Gavi** (light, delicate)
**Vernaccia** (medium, zesty)
**Soave** (medium, zesty)
**Muscat/Moscato** (medium, fruity)
**Vin Santo** (heavy, spicy)
**Vermintino** (medium, zesty)
**Trebbiano** (medium, spicy)
**Greco** (medium, spicy)

# Menus

## Brunch
Bellinis (see *Giada's Family Dinners*)
Breakfast Scramble with Orzo, Pancetta, and Asparagus (page 159)
Goat Cheese Toasts (page 26)
Melon wedges

## Birthday Bash
Mixed Olives
Prosciutto-Wrapped Vegetables with Parmesan (page 39)
Crab Salad Napoleons with Fresh Pasta (page 195)
Insalata Mista with Basil Dressing (page 50)
Birthday cake

## Sunday Afternoon Lunch
Parmesan Popovers (page 31)
Ribollita (page 72)
Insalata Mista with Basil Dressing (page 50)

## Farmer's Market Supper
Anytime Vegetable Salad (page 57)
Capellini Piedmontese (page 138)
Roasted peaches drizzled with Balsamic Syrup (page 28)

## Tailgate Extravaganza
Lemonade
Penne with Beef and Arugula (page 182)
Tuna, Green Bean, and Orzo Salad (page 75)
Zucchini and Carrots a Scapece (page 34)
Watermelon wedges

## Make-Ahead Dinner Party
Crostini with Anchovy Butter and Cheese (page 30)
Salami platter
Roasted artichokes
Baked Penne with Roasted Vegetables (page 89)
Greens with Gorgonzola Dressing (page 53)
Vanilla ice cream with Balsamic Syrup (page 28)

## Wedding Shower Buffet
Prosecco
Asparagus with Vin Santo Vinaigrette (page 55)
Italian Chicken Salad in Lettuce Cups (page 82)
Assorted sorbets

## Kid's Favorite
Fried wontons
Linguine with Turkey Meatballs (page 117)
Steamed broccoli
Canneloni

## Game Night
Cold beer
Fried Zucchini (page 37)
Antipasto platter
Spicy Baked Macaroni (page 191)
Gelato and Italian cookies

## The Day After Thanksgiving
Spinach Salad with Citrus Vinaigrette (page 49)
Turkey and Cranberry Ravioli (page 214)
Leftover pumpkin pie

## Christmas Eve
Neapolitan Calamari and Shrimp Salad (hold the pasta) (page 77)
Crab and Ricotta Manicotti (page 92)
Linguine and Lobster Fra Diavolo (page 209)
Arugula Salad with Fried Gorgonzola (page 46)
Panettone with Vin Santo

## New Year's Eve
Ricotta Gnudi in Parmesan Broth (page 113)
Asparagus with Vin Santo Vinaigrette (page 55)
Champagne Risotto (page 206)
Champagne

## Rainy Day Dinner
Baked Caprese Salad (page 25)
Saffron Orzo with Shrimp (page 127)
Sautéed Spinach with Red Onion (page 56)
Amaretti cookies

# Credits

We are grateful to the companies listed below for the use of their products in this book:

**Sur La Table**
Corporate Headquarters
Seattle Design Center
5701 Sixth Avenue South, Suite 486
Seattle, WA 98108
Store locations nationwide or visit www.surlatable.com

**Maison Midi at American Rag**
148 South La Brea Avenue
Los Angeles, CA 90036
(323) 935-3157

**Anthropologie**
Urban Outfitters, Inc. Corporate Headquarters
1809 Walnut Street
Philadelphia, PA 19103
Retail locations nationwide or visit www.anthropologie.com

**Sointu USA/Global Knives**
Available at www.globalknives.us, or visit www.soituusa.com

# Index